The Prophetic Church

Kjell Sjöberg

New Wine Press

New Wine Press
PO Box 17
Chichester
England
PO20 6YB

Bible quotations, unless otherwise indicated, are from the NIV.
The Holy Bible, New International Version. Copyright © 1973,
1978, New York International Bible Society, published by Hodder
& Stoughton.

RSV Revised Standard Version. © Copyright 1946, 1952 by the
Division of Christian Education of the National Council of the
Churches of Christ in the United States of America.

KJV King James Version.

ISBN: 1 874367 10 8

Typeset by CRB (Drayton) Typesetting Services, Drayton, Norwich.
Printed by Richard Clay Ltd, Bungay, Suffolk.

About the Author

Kjell Sjöberg was born in Stockholm in 1933, the eldest son of six children. His father and grandfather were both Pentecostal ministers. It was at the age of 18 that he came into a first-hand experience of God through faith in Jesus Christ. Six months later, he started to preach. At the age of 23 he planted his first church in Sweden. In 1961 he went to Pakistan with his wife Lena, and together they worked there for 11 years, planting churches and starting the Full Gospel Bible School in Lahore. After returning to Sweden in 1972, he started a church in Järfälla, a suburb of Stockholm, which in ten years grew to 650 members.

For ten years he was a leader of Intercessors for Sweden. Since 1983 he has ministered in many countries in all the continents, leading prayer journeys, teaching about prayer and particularly prayer war, and working with prayer movements praying for cities and nations. He also takes a leading part in the prayer movement in his native Stockholm.

He has written a number of books in the Swedish language, and his first book to be made available in English, *Winning the Prayer War* (1991), sold over 4,000 copies in its first year of publication.

During his brief periods at home, Kjell Sjöberg lives at Bro, near Stockholm, with his wife Lena, where they share their family life with their son Samuel, his wife and five grandchildren, who live next door.

Contents

Foreword

'See, I will send you the prophet Elijah before that great and dreadful day of the LORD comes.'   (Malachi 4:5)

It is a great privilege for me to write an introduction to this book. I have known Kjell Sjöberg for a number of years, learning so much from him. We have worked closely together in many conferences on prayer, intercession and spiritual warfare.

These are tremendous times in which we live. Never before has a generation been privileged to see so much of God's word being fulfilled before their eyes. It is a time of unparalleled shaking. As we observe the nations, it is difficult to find one which remains untouched.

'At that time His voice shook the earth, but now He has promised, "Once more I will shake not only the earth but also the heavens." The words "once more" indicate the removing of what can be shaken – that is, created things – so that what cannot be shaken may remain.'
(Hebrews 12:26–27)

Without question, God is the author of the shaking process and He knows what He is doing. More than anything else, He is in the business of refining His body – the Church. These humanly insoluble crises demand a Church that is ready for prophetic action in this last hour of the present age and God will not be denied. This shaking has a twofold purpose, to prepare a prophetic people who, in turn, will prepare the way for the return of the Lord Jesus in glory.

A prophetic Church is pre-requisite for a prophetic age. I personally believe that this generation will see the return of the Lord Jesus to Jerusalem where He will establish His kingdom *'on earth as it is in heaven.'* In these exciting days, it has been our privilege to participate with the Lord in the return of Jewish people back to the Promised Land. This, too, is part of the Elijah ministry. The context of the *'voice crying in the wilderness'* is a ministry dedicated to the comfort of God's chosen people.

This makes *The Prophetic Church* a very timely book highlighting the underlying causes and true nature of the evils that beset our societies and threaten our very civilisation. We are assured that the Bible does have the answers and provides the chart and compass needed to steer us victoriously through the tempest of the last days of this age. Therefore, let us turn to God as never before to seek His face on behalf of ourselves, our homes, our church, our nation, the nation and people of Israel and our world.

The book of James reminds us that *'Elijah was a man just like us'* and God is seeking those who will be part of this collective ministry which is the prophetic Church. Kjell Sjöberg has been a pioneer and God is using him and his teaching ministry, in the last days, to be a part of the preparation for the return of the Lord Jesus. For in that day, *'the Bride will have made herself ready.'* Amen.

Gustav Scheller
October 1992

Chapter 1

The Prophetic Church

The special role of the prophetic Church in the End Time

The End Time will inevitably be prophetic, because there is so much prophecy from God's Word that has yet to be fulfilled. So the Church needs to be prophetic in order to be able to keep its sense of direction in a time of chaos. In a period of great changes and transitions, when God's people enter the pilgrim stage, the voices of prophecy become particularly important.

I believe in a restored and triumphant Church, and in the restoration of a prophetic ministry, in the End Time. I believe there will be a prophetic Church before Jesus returns. By a prophetic Church, I mean a Church that acts corporately as the Old Testament prophets used to do. In these days, the Lord is not going to be using special prophet figures, separate from the main Body of Christ. I believe in single individuals as prophetic voices, but functioning together with the whole Church, so that the whole Body becomes involved in the course of events.

Elijah's prophetic ministry in the End Time

Elijah was a prophet whose message has a vital connection with the close of this age. One of the principles of the old Jewish interpretation of Scripture was that the miracles of Elijah's time, and God's intervention in the earlier history of the Jewish people, followed a prophetic pattern, which is going to be repeated in the End Time, but on a wider scale. This principle is the background to Malachi's prophecy that the prophet Elijah will come back before the great and dreadful day of the Lord. In this book, we shall be studying the life and the prophetic ministry of Elijah in order to find the parallels with the respective roles of the individual, the Church, and of Israel, in the End Time.

The theme of this book grew in part out of a course of teaching that I was following in the Pentecostal church at Järfälla, near Stockholm, during my time as pastor there in 1981. It also originated partly from an intercession campaign for Sweden initiated by the group called Intercessors for Sweden. Each year in our church at Järfälla we used to have a principal theme for the whole year's teaching. At the beginning of the year, I wrote an introduction to the theme for the year, and set out our goals of faith for the spiritual growth of the church. The following is an extract from this material.

Goals of faith concerning the prophetic Church

'Because many people in our time have lost faith in the future, and are suffering from a sense of catastrophe, we want to proclaim the overflowing hope in Christ that comes from a deeper understanding of the teaching of the Bible about the last times.

'This prophetic word will be put in focus in the church's teaching during 1981. This means that we shall be studying the books of Revelation and Daniel.

'A deeper understanding of the prophetic word will lead the church into becoming the light, the salt, the city on a hill, the church that keeps a step ahead, and has the courage to act within the framework of the prophetic word.

'The hope of God's kingdom will enable us to live prophetically in the present time.

'Our goal of faith is to awaken the prophetic conscience of every member of the church, so that we can give to one another prophetic information, and live in a prophetic fellowship, that is, the alternative society with a life-style appropriate to the next age.

'Our study of the End Time is not to be carried out in order to satisfy our curiosity, but with the purpose of bringing in the kingdom of God on earth.'

The prophetic Church studies the prophetic word in order to know its true way through the dreary wilderness of the present age, and to have the goal of God's kingdom clearly in view (2 Peter 1:19–21).

The Church is built on the foundation of the prophets (Ephesians 2:21). Who were these prophets, who laid the foundation of the Church? They were, amongst others, those apostles who also had a prophetic ministry; for example John, Peter and Paul. It was in the capacity of apostles that they laid the foundation of the local churches, and began the building of the Church itself. But they never saw the completion of the whole Temple, nor have we seen it yet. They saw the finished Temple in prophetic visions, and they saw what the Church would have to go through before reaching its final goal. We are a Church that is incomplete. We have much more building-up to do. Therefore, we must seek to know the overall design of the prophets for the future, so that we can build God's House so securely that it will not fall when the last great storm breaks over the world. When the foundations of the earth start shaking, then the Church will be the pillar and foundation of the truth (1 Timothy 3:15).

What is the prophetic word? I would like to define it as the teaching of Jesus and the apostles about the last things, which is found throughout the New Testament, and also what the prophets of the Old Testament have spoken.

The following is the list of chapters and books of Scripture which I suggested the church should study during that year, 1981:

Matthew 24 and 25
Luke 17 and 21
Mark 13
Romans 9–11
2 Timothy 3 and 4
1 Thessalonians 4 and 5
2 Thessalonians 1 and 2
2 Peter 3
1 John 2 and 4
Revelation
Daniel

When we formed the concept of 'the prophetic Church', we did not fully realise what that expression stood for. It was not a complete concept for us, but an idea that awakened our curiosity and helped us, during the year, to give form and content to it. In the previous year (1980) the theme had been 'Discovering gifts', and having stated that as the theme, we had gone on to fill it out and give it content through the process that took place in the church. We trusted that a process of growth would take place, both through the teaching itself and through putting it into practice in our own lives, and through this same kind of process we expected in turn to give content and meaning to the expression 'the prophetic Church'.

The Church with a prophetic responsibility and prophetic information

In the contexts where I have seen or heard the expression 'the prophetic Church' used, it has generally served to show the church's responsibility in the community and in the nation. My friend Paul Liljenberg spoke at a meeting of pastors concerning:

1. The traditional Church, which has a message of consolation and salvation for the private individual;
2. The modernised Church, which adapts its methods of activity and takes account of modern movements, for instance, church growth, and so on;

3. The prophetic Church, which through its life of fellowship seeks to present the response of God's kingdom in the community.

Bob Mumford has spoken of the prophetic Church in connection with the response of intercession for the nation, when the Church has assumed the role that the Old Testament prophets had. Those prophets were the conscience of the nation; they drew attention to the national sins; they gave proper warning when they realised that the community was under the judgment of God; they showed the way when the nation stood at various crossroads. The prophets had to choose and anoint the leaders of their country, and to encourage them and give them direction, but they also had to warn and pronounce judgement over those leaders who broke God's laws. The prophets were the bearers of visions of the future for the people. In the New Testament, it is the Body of Christ that is to fulfil the office of prophet in the community and the nation. The prophets are to be part of the leadership of the Church, and the prophetic gift is to be an important part of the Body, used frequently and belonging to the whole Body. When these gifts are in use, they help the whole Church to live and act prophetically.

The church described in Acts was prophetic, when it interpreted the various experiences through which it was passing in the light of the prophetic word. On the day of Pentecost, Peter was able to interpret the pouring out of the Holy Spirit as the fulfilment of Joel's prophecy. The persecution in Jerusalem was only what was described in Psalm 2 as a rebellion against Christ (Acts 4:24–28). At the council meeting of the apostles in Jerusalem, James was able to stand up and interpret the course of events that had led to Gentiles becoming Christians, as a fulfilment of the prophecy of Amos that the Gentiles would bear the name of the Lord (Acts 15:14–18). They saw what was happening in the Church as a fulfilment of prophecy.

In Antioch, the whole church became involved in acting according to prophetic information. Agabus announced, by inspiration of the Spirit, that there would be a severe famine.

> *'The disciples, each according to his ability, decided to provide help for the brothers living in Judea. This they did, sending their gift to the elders by Barnabas and Saul.'*
>
> (Acts 11:27–30)

Here the whole church was prophetic, as the prophetic message led them all into acting in a practical way.

When Paul, as a prisoner, was taken on that troubled voyage over the Mediterranean, he was constantly kept informed by the Lord. When they were sailing along the coast of Crete, Paul was able to warn the ship's captain:

> *'I can see that our voyage is going to be disastrous and bring great loss to ship and cargo, and to our own lives also.'*
>
> (Acts 27:10–11)

But no one took any notice of this first warning from Paul. Later in the voyage, they did listen to him (Acts 27:21–26).

The Old Testament prophets gave prophetic information both to individuals and to the nation. They were friends of God and therefore they came to know God's secrets (Amos 3:7). The friends of Jesus stand in the same confidential relationship and can thus also know God's secrets (John 15:15). Samuel was able to give prophetic information and instruction to Saul (1 Samuel 10:1–8). Jeremiah was able to give prophetic information to those living in captivity in Babylon, showing them what they should do in order to survive the captivity, and how long they would remain in Babylon (Jeremiah 38:14–23; 39:1–7).

How can the Body of Christ, with its many members, fulfil the same task as a single person? We can all prophesy (1 Corinthians 14:31–32). We are exhorted eagerly to desire the gift of prophecy (1 Corinthians 14:1–5). But when a number of people prophesy, not every one of them knows the whole plan of God. The Lord gives to each one a share of the information. Each prophet receives a piece, a fragment (1 Corinthians 13:9). This means that God does not reveal everything to one single prophet, but he allows him only to see a glimpse of his overall plan. Unity and fellowship among the prophets is needed in order for us to learn the whole counsel of God. It is as a Church in unity that we receive the whole measure of information.

God's plan for survival in times of trouble lies in the prophetic Church. Demos Shakarian tells how a prophet foretold the persecution that would come against the Christians in his home village of Kara Kala in Armenia. The prophet foresaw a tragedy in which a hundred thousand people would be killed. He urged them to be ready to flee one day. They obtained a map of the flight journey, which terminated on the east coast of the United States, but they were told to continue their journey to the west coast of this new country. There, God would bless them and give them success. Fifty years later, the boy prophet, now grown up, announced that the time had now come when the vision would become reality. 'Flee to America! Everyone who stays behind will be killed.' A group of Pentecostal families obeyed the prophetic instruction. In 1914 there began a time of terror and suffering for the Armenian people, in which two-thirds of them, over a million, were killed, including all the Christians from the village of Kara Kala. Demos Shakarian's grandfather sold his farm in 1905 in obedience to the prophetic information he had received, thereby saving his family.

The prophetic Church prepares for its special role and task in the last times

This can imply quickly putting the economic resources of the Church at the disposal of a great missionary offensive, with hordes of workers going out bearing the final invitation to come to Christ before the time of God's wrath breaks out.

It can also be concerned with the special role of the Church in the salvation of the Jews.

It can also mean living in that special state of vigilance that is required before the reign of Antichrist begins, when he comes and demands the loyalty of the people of God.

When we study the prophetic word, we find that there are special instructions for the Christians of the last generation, who will join in meeting the Lord Jesus at his coming.

The prophetic Church dares to act within the framework of the prophetic word

We are not given the prophetic word as a programme to enable us to sit in the spectator's seat and follow what is going on down in the arena. On the contrary, we find ourselves in the arena itself, where we need the prophetic programme in order to know how we are to act in accordance with God's will. We receive the prophetic word so that we ourselves can be part of the fulfilment of that word.

The prophetic Church will carry out what needs to be done in order to bring Jesus back to the earth

In the Old Testament, we can see how many individual people worked together to bring Jesus to this world the first time. Ruth's declaration of loyalty to Naomi was an act of this kind, bringing her into the line of Jesus' ancestors. Boaz took his responsibility as kinsman-redeemer for Naomi and Ruth, which brought him also into the Messianic line. It was not only Joseph and Mary who cooperated so as to bring Jesus into the world. Samuel was also a link in the chain, when he went to anoint David as king.

In the same way, the Church and individual people can take their part in the process of bringing Jesus back.

> *'Since everything will be destroyed in this way, what kind of people ought you to be? You ought to live holy and godly lives as you look forward to the day of God and speed its coming.'* (2 Peter 3:11–12)

The Church contributes to the destruction of all things in the last times, by going in the opposite direction in its development towards holy and godly living. This polarisation will speed the coming of the day of God.

The Characteristics of the Prophetic Church

This extract is a summary of a section entitled 'The Prophetic Role' in Howard Snyder's book *The Community of the King*, published in 1977. He gives the following four characteristics of the Church in fulfilling its prophetic function:

1. *The Church is prophetic when it creates and sustains a reconciled and reconciling community of believers*. 2 Corinthians 5:16–21; Colossians 1:21–23; Philippians 2:1–11; Ephesians 2:1–22.

All division must be seen as sin and worldliness: 1 Corinthians 3:3–4. In the local Church, reconciliation must be more than a theory and more than an invisible spiritual transaction. Reconciliation must be real and visible, so that all divisions between men on grounds of race, economic differences, or elitism must be challenged biblically. The local church should work to reconcile marriage partners, parents and children, employer and employee, whenever there is discord in these relationships. Above all, the Church must be a demonstration of this reconciliation within its own community, and then it can exercise a continuing ministry of reconciliation in the world.

2. *The Church is prophetic when it recognises and identifies the true enemy*. Matthew 10:28; Luke 12:4–5; Ephesians 6:12; Romans 8:38–39; 1 Corinthians 15:26; Revelation 20:2.

The Church has often been deceived into taking sides in a conflict without discerning who the true enemy is. Satan wants us to accept a substitute god and a counterfeit enemy. He does not want to be the target himself. There are many false definitions of the problem, and the nature of man is that he always prefers to blame someone other than himself. At various periods in history, the Church has been deceived into warring against false arch-enemies: Turks, Saracens, insubordination to the hierarchy, re-baptism, the Jews, black people, white people, Nazism, Communism, Capitalism, Imperialism. When the Church accepts Satan's false definition of the enemy, it also readily accepts Satan's tactics. The Church must define the true enemy in the spirit realm that lies behind the visible enemy.

17

3. *The Church is prophetic when it renounces the world's definition and practice of power*. Matthew 20:20–28; 23:1–12; Mark 9:35–37; Luke 9:46–48; 22:24–27; John 13:12–17; Philippians 2:1–11; 1 Corinthians 1:18–31.

Power in the Church is not a question of position or hierarchy or titles; it is a question of function and of service. The greatness of a Christian is not according to office, status, degrees or reputation, but according to how he or she functions as a servant. The world is deluded. It believes that real power is a matter of politics. As Jacques Ellul has said, 'There is a kind of cloud of confusion surrounding politics, a political obsession according to which nothing has significance or importance apart from political intervention and, when all is said and done, all issues are political.' This attitude is a political myth, to which the Church also falls prey. The Church must reject all attempts to make politics, or the state, ultimate or sacred.

The spiritual armour for prayer war. (Ephesians 6:13–18)	**The weapons of the flesh used by the world.**
(a) The belt of truth buckled round your waist – truth without compromise.	Propaganda, truth twisted for political ends. In propaganda, truth is not sacred, but only a tool to be used.
(b) The armour of righteousness.	Violence and oppression, which the world calls justice. In human warfare, righteousness is always a victim.
(c) The gospel of peace.	The gospel of power.
(d) The shield of faith.	The shield of ideology, a false faith leading to total commitment to false gods.
(e) The helmet of salvation.	A false, this-worldly Utopia.

18

(f) The sword of God's Word.	Human sources of revelation such as science, technology, philosophy, or a false messiah (whether political or religious).
(g) Prayer.	Effective action.

4. *The Church is prophetic when it works for justice in society.* Psalm 82:1–4; Amos 5:21–24; Luke 3:10–14; 4:18–21; Matthew 11:4–6; Ephesians 5:11.

Christians bear a particular responsibility to the poor and oppressed. The treatment of the poor, the needy, and those who have no social or political power becomes a test of the degree of justice prevailing in any society or political system. Therefore it is also a test of the Church's true concept of justice.

The Church's prophetic Kingdom tasks

The Church is prophetic when it is truly the messianic community which reveals the nature of the Kingdom and the mind and stature of Jesus Christ. As it carries on the work of Christ it fulfils its Kingdom tasks.

But this will never be a neat, clear-cut, triumphant road for the Church to follow. Obedience to the Gospel in a world where Satan is still active means living with tension. We, as Christians, can never be sure we have all the answers or are really making progress. We are therefore constantly forced back to total dependence on Jesus. We should be alarmed if we find ourselves at home in the world, or if we have total peace of mind. The Christian life in a non-Christian world means tension, stress and agony. A whole system of social techniques aims to adjust the individual to the world and to eliminate tensions. But being a follower of Jesus means accepting the scandal of Jesus' statements that he came to bring not harmony but discord; not peace, but a sword (Matthew 10:34–36).

As society becomes more and more godless, the Church must increasingly see itself as, and in practice structure itself deliberately to become, a counter-culture. This is necessary to enable the Church to be true to the Gospel and its prophetic role in the world.

In summary, the Church's Kingdom tasks include the proclamation of the Gospel in such a way that men and women respond in faith and obedience to Jesus and join in building the Christian community. This community is a new social reality which, through its likeness to Christ and its renunciation of the world's definitions and tactics, reveals the true nature of God's reign. 'The Lord calls and continues to call out a new society of persons unconditionally committed to exchanging the values of the surrounding society for the standards of Jesus' kingdom.' Only on this basis can the Church work as a reliable platform for justice and peace in the world. Thus the prophetic and evangelistic dimensions of the Gospel are totally interwoven with the life and witness of the community of the King. Through this community there comes into being an alternative society, which completely separates itself from the culture of this age.

The Alternative Society

The book of Daniel gives an example of how a small colony of the kingdom of heaven was formed in Babylon through Daniel and his three friends. It was a close fellowship having its own life-style. They lived in a fellowship of prayer, and became a team in which various gifts grew up: the gift of wisdom and the gift of interpretation. Daniel interpreted dreams, and became a prophet, while his friends supported him with a prayer ministry. Together they experienced God's protection, and contributed together to the kingdom of God, thereby changing the community and the attitude of the king of Babylon.

Daniel and his friends became the counter-culture of the kingdom of God in Babylon. Through their fellowship and the protection given to them by God, they were able to survive their time of captivity and to emerge victorious.

I have sought to find a key word suited to each chapter of the book of Daniel, a word that describes the kingdom of this world. Then I have looked for the corresponding word from the Bible that expresses the response of the kingdom of God to that key word in each case.

Chapter 1: Instead of *indoctrination* according to this world, we believe in a spiritual community which nurtures *spiritual maturity*.

Chapter 2: Instead of *destruction*, we are to live in *restoration*.

Chapter 3: Instead of worshipping *false gods*, we are to worship *the only true God*.

Chapter 4: Instead of *pride*, our personality is to be characterised by *humility*.

Chapter 5: Instead of *blasphemy*, we declare God to be *holy*.

Chapter 6: Instead of *jealousy* and *intrigue*, the kingdom of God is *love* and *encouragement*.

Chapter 7: Instead of the nature of a *wild animal*, the kingdom of God confers on us the nature of *the Lamb*.

Chapter 8: Instead of *rebellion*, God's kingdom is one of *obedience* and *submission*.

Chapter 9: Instead of *cursing*, God's kingdom substitutes the ministry of *intercession*.

Chapter 10: Instead of the *spirit principalities* of the kingdom of darkness, we work together with the *angels* in the kingdom of light.

Chapter 11: Instead of the *powers of chaos*, we are to live in the *kingdom of peace*.

Chapter 12: Instead of *desolation*, we believe in *resurrection*.

The Church – a community in miniature

The Church is to be the city on the hill that Jesus talked of. We have been living through a development that has led to more and more of the cares and concerns of family life being offloaded on to the community. We pay high taxes so that officials can do the things that used to be looked after by relatives, or by the small farm community. Looking after children during the day, which used to be done by the older folk, is now handed over to the nursery school. The elderly are put into an old people's home instead of staying as part of the enlarged family. Perhaps the time has come to reverse this process and gradually to take back into our own hands the care of one another, instead of handing it all over to the state or the local council.

The Bible teaches us the right priority in our caring. First and foremost, our care should be for our nearest brothers and sisters.

> *'Therefore, as we have opportunity, let us do good to all people, especially to those who belong to the family of believers.'*　　　　　　　　　　　　　　　　(Galatians 6:10)

I would like to translate this to apply to those situated nearest to us in, for example, our prayer group.

Paul followed this principle during his year spent in Ephesus (Acts 20:34–35). Paul worked as a tent-maker, first in order to earn his own living, secondly to support his team, his fellow-workers, and thirdly to care for the weak. We have often run away from the needs of our nearest brothers, because we thought the need in other lands was greater, but by doing so we have lost the strength of our impact on the world. We have turned away from the idea of a *'city on a hill'* (Matthew 5:14–16).

Release creative imagination in the Christian community!

In one charismatic fellowship, described by Elizabeth O'Connor in *The Eighth Day of Creation*, role-playing was used in mission groups to help individuals to discover the gifts that could be used for mission work. The group had a time of silence when they were asked to use their imagination to find out their gifts and roles to play in a mission team. The result was that they learned that when their imaginings were brought out into the open, people dared to bring out ideas that they had nursed for some time but had never dared to express.

When what we say does not bind us to a long-term commitment, and we are not under pressure to succeed or to please others, we are free to experiment and explore outlandish possibilities. Eric Hoffer says, 'Many inventions had their birth as toys ... Such crucial instruments as the telescope and the microscope were first conceived as play-things.'

Why then should we not also be able to make discoveries in God's kingdom by releasing our creative imagination? How would a prayer group be able to survive on a desert island? Who would do what in that situation? How would the prayer group manage to take over and run a farm together? Could we start a project together? What kind of farming would we be able to do? Is there anyone in the group harbouring some vision which needs several people to carry it into reality? Can we imagine together how we would be able to realise that vision? How would we allocate the various roles? How would we allot the different parts, if we were to produce a play together? Is there some need within the group, or in our neighbourhood area, which we can go some way to meeting by working together? What has our stocktaking of the different gifts shown us?

How has 'the prophetic Church' worked out in practice?

I have described earlier in this chapter how during 1981, in the church that I was leading in a Stockholm suburb, we carried out a teaching programme. We concentrated particularly on the books of Revelation and Daniel. One of the pastors taught from the letters to the Thessalonians in a series of 'Bring the Word' meetings on Sunday mornings, and I myself taught from the prophetic passages in 2 Timothy 3–4 and Matthew 24–25. We worked in this way all through the year without a break, teaching about the last things, finding out how the Church should truly be, and how it should prepare itself for its part in the End Time.

Towards the end of the year, the vision of a restored, triumphant Church in the End Time had become stronger, while I, from God's Word, came to know more about increased pressure from the powers of darkness, and the Bible's description of the End Time as a time of chaos and destruction.

During the year, we experienced what Howard Snyder had been writing about when he described the Christian life in a non-Christian world, in the passage summarised earlier, as meaning tension, stress and agony; a Church appointed not to bring peace, but a sword.

The prophetic Church is by nature in conflict with the frightened Church. There is a great deal of fear about the future. As we develop our prophetic function, tension with the religious forms increases. The traditional Church with its traditional roles of pastor, church member, choir member, appears more and more clumsy.

Our church came together in prophetic action when many members took part, with other believers, in a day of prayer in Sergels Torg, a large square in the centre of Stockholm, on 1st May 1981. A Swedish-American brother, Bill Lövbom, had seen in a vision, six months earlier, several thousand Christians coming together and praying in front of the Parliament building. We wondered at first whether Pentecost Sunday might be a better time than 1st May, but Bill was sure of the date the Lord had given him. We sensed that Sweden would perhaps be in the middle of a crisis of some kind at the time. We were right. On 1st May that year, Sweden was without a government. The previous coalition government had resigned, and we found it most significant to have so many praying at that moment.

In order to give the whole picture of 'the prophetic Church' at that time, I must also mention that several people in the church found the preaching from Revelation to be hard going. Criticism in the Christian press was directed against the church, on the lines that it was paying more attention to the Antichrist than to Christ, even though we were seeking hard to know what the Lord wanted us to do in order to hasten his coming to reign over the world.

The campaign of intercession during the election year, 1982

In every election year, the organisation 'Intercessors for Sweden' used to arrange prayer days throughout the country. At the end of 1981 we appointed a day for seeking prophetic information for our strategy for 1982. Five of us leaders from Intercessors for Sweden met together one Wednesday from midday till 9 pm. During that time, the elders of my own local church held a prayer watch, for an hour each by turns, asking the Lord to reveal his strategy. During the day, we also had telephone contact with others who had been asked beforehand to take part with us in seeking the Lord's will. If any of these people had any leading, they were to ring us, and many of them did so.

We prayed over many areas of the life of our country that needed to be lifted to the Lord in prayer. The particular matters that were brought out as topics for prayer were:

1. The family situation in Sweden. The attacks against the family come from many directions, and many forces are working to destroy it.
2. Sweden's attitude to Israel.
3. The responsibility for interceding for the nation.
4. Economic crime. Dishonesty over state benefits, shoplifting, tax evasion. This kind of crime, in greater or lesser form, forces the community into increased official control.
5. Anti-Christian tendencies in the community.
6. The community's neutrality in the face of different forms of living together, and in the face of non-Christian religions. Sweden is historically a Christian country, and we should pray that politicians who are not Christians should nevertheless honour our land's Christian foundations. We believe in freedom of religion, but not in religious neutrality.
7. National unity instead of strong confrontation between political groups, social classes, and groups with special interests.
8. The occult movement.

When we could see more closely the connection between these various prayer topics, we saw that each one of them was associated with some aspect of the ministry of the prophet Elijah:

1. Elijah had a ministry of turning the hearts of members of the family to one another.
2. Elijah caused Israel to make a decision on Mount Carmel.
3. Elijah took responsibility as an intercessor for the nation.
4. Elijah took a stand against economic crime (Naboth's vineyard).
5. Elijah confronted Ahab, a king who opposed God.
6. Elijah challenged the politics of neutrality, 'limping between two opinions'.
7. When Elijah built up the broken-down altar, he did it as a proclamation of the nation's unity.
8. Elijah held a king responsible for seeking help from occult sources instead of from the Lord.

All the prayer topics which arose in our gathering were areas to which Elijah had been directed. Our prayer strategy took as its governing principle, 'Exercising an Elijah ministry in Sweden'.

During the months of April and May, we visited about twenty places, where we gathered all the people of God in prayer and applied the ministry of Elijah, in proclamation and in seeking to motivate people in the light of the various areas for prayer. On the Swedish national day, 6th June, we held another day of prayer in Sergels Torg in front of the Parliament building. When we prayed for Israel, we invited the Israeli Ambassador to be present and to speak.

This book grew out of that day of prayer, when we sought a strategy for our country, and also out of what we lived through during our two months of holding prayer days all over Sweden.

Chapter 2

'I Will Send You the Prophet Elijah'

The Old Testament ends with the prophecy that the Lord will send the prophet Elijah, before the great and dreadful day of the Lord comes (Malachi 4:5–6).

Jesus confirms this prophecy by saying:

> *'To be sure, Elijah comes and will restore all things. But I tell you, Elijah has already come.'* (Matthew 17:11)

Jesus' words mean that Elijah has come, but they also mean that he is going to come. If Jesus is speaking the truth, then Elijah's coming must be seen in several different persons.

Elijah came back through Elisha continuing his life's work in the spirit of Elijah.

Elijah came back through John the Baptist, who went before Jesus in the spirit and power of Elijah (Luke 1:17).

Elijah returns through intercessors who pray as Elijah prayed. According to James, Elijah can come back all over the world in the Christian church through those who pray (James 5:17–18).

The Jews have a strong expectation of Elijah. Every year when they celebrate the Passover in their homes, they place an empty chair, 'Elijah's chair', ready at the table, in case Elijah should suddenly appear as a guest in their home. There is a great need for many to serve in the spirit and power of Elijah, to fill all those empty chairs.

It may be that the prophecy about the return of Elijah

ultimately refers to a particular person with a prophetic mission to Israel. But that which God does now, always stands in context with what he has done earlier. He has called out his Church for a special mission for the end of this present age. It is my belief that the Bride-Church will also be the prophetic Church, characterised by Elijah's prophetic ministry. The Elijah ministry, then, is fulfilled by many different people.

This book is written from the point of view that the Elijah ministry is highly relevant and appropriate to describe the Church's role in the End Time.

Before the Old Testament prophets came forward, they heard the Lord roaring like a lion. *'The Lord roars from Zion'* (Amos 1:2). What was the Lord saying, that he roared like a lion? 'My spirit roars after the prophet Elijah', said the Lord in a vision to a Dutch preacher, Abraham Leenhouts. God's Spirit thirsts after someone who will stand in the gap with responsibility for the land (Ezekiel 22:30). God's Spirit thirsts after individual people of God who will undertake prophet-service in the End Time with responsibility for the land, so that he will not need to strike the land with a curse.

Elijah – God's restored man

Suddenly, Elijah comes forward. The first time we read about him, he stands before King Ahab (1 Kings 17:1). Ahab and Elijah are complete opposites to one another. Ahab is a man who has done more to provoke the Lord to anger than anyone else before him (1 Kings 16:30–34; 21:25). He is the anti-God man, who gave himself over entirely to the service of idols. He is the man of apostasy. Elijah, on the other hand, is God's restored man. These two men, totally opposed to one another, stand face to face, but there is a connection between them. The whole of creation strives for equilibrium. Water takes a position of equilibrium. When the apostate, anti-God man, comes forward, the whole creation strives after equilibrium with the result that the man of God is raised up to stand in opposition to him. Thus Elijah came forward at the time of greatest darkness, at the Antichrist-time, as a type, an example of the man that God brings forward. Times of darkness and trouble produce such exemplary men of God.

Before the return of Jesus, there will again be times of trouble, of birth-pains, times when everything will disintegrate. The balance then demands the opposite course of things – times of restoration. In our own time there are psychologists who purposely work with the aim of wiping out man's image of God. They succeed too in bringing forth the complete, secularised man, with the image of God obliterated. But from this destroyed image of God, there emerges the face of Satan. At this time, we shall also come to see men and women bearing the visible image of God, men and women who resemble Christ.

Elijah must come, in order to restore all things (Matthew 17:11). But first, he must himself be raised up. The Bible's concept of restoration implies a bringing back of everything to its original state, just as God had created it at the beginning. Restoration means recovering one's freedom, recovering one's inheritance. When the Year of Jubilee was proclaimed in Israel, there was a restoration, a reconveyance of lost family property. Elijah comes forward in this way before Ahab, as one who has received back the lost family inheritance of Adam.

1. Elijah has a restored relationship with God. He knows that he is the servant of the Lord. He knows the Lord and he knows his will.

2. Elijah appears as the Lord's representative, the Lord's agent with full powers to act on his behalf. He derives his authority from the Lord. It was in the same way that Adam, before his fall, was appointed to have dominion over the creation.

3. Elijah has authority over the created world. He intervenes in the weather pattern and stops the rain, until Ahab and the people are ready to stand before the Lord on Carmel. Elijah's right to interfere with nature was also a right given to Adam (Genesis 1:28).

4. Elijah has a highly-developed prayer life. He expresses in his prayer that which God afterwards carries out. When he prays, the Lord's word is in his mouth (1 Kings 17:21–24). Elijah undertook responsibility for the nation in his

prayer. When he prayed that it would not rain for three and a half years, such a prayer affected the entire nation. He challenged the whole anti-God state by means of a sign, given to him by God, so as to carry the whole people forward to the point of decision.

5. Elijah is equipped with spiritual gifts. He has the gift of working miracles, and the gift of prophecy. The restored man or woman is a temple of the Holy Spirit, and the gifts of the Spirit will operate through him or her.

Those who are restored, as the result of redemption by Jesus, become rehabilitated people in the same way as Elijah. Elijah is not merely a unique example of a man of God, but is the prototype of the restored human being, who has received back everything that all of us once lost. It is from this that I derive my belief that in the last times there will be a large number of Elijahs.

The signs of the kingdom of God in the restored man

1. *Elijah was in harmony with the created world*. For him, the physical world was part of his protection. The Lord gave him the order to go and hide himself in the Kerith ravine. There he was supplied with fresh water during the period of drought, and the ravens brought him bread and meat (1 Kings 17:3–6).

John the Baptist, also an Elijah-man, was in harmony with the created world in a different way. He lived in the desert, but found everything he needed in nature. He wore clothing made of camel-hair, with a leather belt round his waist, and he ate locusts and wild honey (Mark 1:6). Jesus lived in the desert with the wild animals (Mark 1:13). An angel warns the people of God during the time of the Antichrist to worship him who made the springs of water (Revelation 14:6–7). So at that time there will be a need for streams like Kerith. To worship the Creator and to live in his ordered creation is a protection for man (Romans 1:20–21).

2. *Elijah learnt to live in the Lord's unlimited resources*. At the home of the widow in Zarephath, he underwent a long-continued miracle of provision of food, as God blessed the oil and the flour, so that they were not used up. It may have been

as long as three years, that he and the widow experienced a new miracle of God every meal-time (1 Kings 17:8–16).

The two witnesses who come forward in the headquarters of the Antichrist are also marked with an Elijah ministry. They, by their acts, show the same signs as Elijah and Moses, standing in an unbroken flow of the Spirit's power (Revelation 11:3–6).

These signs of God's kingdom were found in Elisha too (2 Kings 4:42–44). Jesus was the totally restored man, and we can see the same signs in him. Jesus lived in the superabundance of God; he was able to pour out of God's limitless resources, both to satisfy his own needs and also to minister to the needs of others. He blessed the five loaves and the two small fish, so that they fed thousands.

3. *Elijah was served by angels*. During his flight from Jezebel, Elijah was on two occasions awakened by an angel, who served him with food and drink (1 Kings 19:4–8). Jesus was served by angels (Mark 1:13). Elisha, who continued Elijah's ministry, was given the protection of an angelic army when he was surrounded by the army of the enemy (2 Kings 6:14–17).

These three Kingdom signs were privileges accorded also to Adam when he lived in the garden of Eden. While he remained in harmony with God's creation, all his needs were supplied by what the Lord provided for him, while the garden was protected by angels, of whom we later read that after the Fall they continued to guard it, so that Adam would not be able to return there.

The last times, before the return of Jesus, are going to be so hard for those who are determined to stand outside the economic system of Antichrist, that it will be necessary for all these signs of God's kingdom to be in evidence so that the Church can go through those times in victory.

Elijah recaptured the experiences that the people of Israel had gone through during their wandering in the desert, when they were provided with manna, when the Lord sent them quails so that they would have meat to eat, and when the angel of the Lord was sent to guard them along the way. The people in Elijah's time had lost faith in God's fatherly care, so they worshipped Baal, a fertility god, to make themselves rich and successful. Before they could release their grasp on the fertility god, Elijah had to redirect their thinking towards God's fatherly care, so that the people would dare to rely on it.

God's people thrive in dark times

When does the restored man of God step forward? We have established that he comes forward in times of darkness. In our conception, we have often assumed that we will reach maturity after our death, or after the coming of Jesus. By this error we have made ourselves comfortable and have left ourselves in a state of inadequate spiritual growth. We have been content with the spiritually immature condition of the Christian Church, assuring ourselves that it will all come out right in the end after we die.

When Jesus was on the mountain of the transfiguration, Elijah and Moses appeared in glory and talked with Jesus about his approaching departure (Luke 9:28–31). Elijah and Moses were being consulted as experts on departure; Jesus needed such people so that he could talk and share experiences with them. The struggle that Moses and Elijah had been through was like the resistance that Jesus met from the Sanhedrin. Elijah could share with Jesus all his experiences that led up to his ascension into heaven. Moses had led the Exodus from Egypt, which in many ways resembled Jesus' departure from this world.

Both of them had undergone experiences during their earthly lives that were like those that Jesus would be going through in Jerusalem. So Elijah and Moses were both able to give richly from their store of experience, in their conversation with Jesus. Peter, James and John, who were with Jesus on the mountain, were still only at the children's stage, and could not therefore meet the need that Jesus had, to talk with someone about the depth of God's purposes concerning his departure.

Paul in Ephesians 4 talks of the building-up of the body of Christ, to bring the people of God to the same spiritual stature as that which Moses and Elijah had when they spoke with Jesus on the mountain of transfiguration. We will grow up into him who is the Head; we will grow to maturity, to the whole measure of the fullness of Christ (Ephesians 4:12–15). When did Elijah and Moses undergo those experiences that enabled them to be partners in conversation with Jesus? Were they before or after Moses' death? Were they before or after Elijah's ascension? They were before, in each case, while they were still on earth. In this way they became men of God. We have transferred too much of our hope over to the other side, and therefore have up to now missed much of the spiritual growth that God has wanted in our lives here and now, while we are on earth. In the darkest times, at the close of this age, Jesus will bring his church into maturity.

A complete man of God

Paul speaks of men of God when he speaks of the last times (2 Timothy 3:16–17). He describes difficult times in the last days, a falling-away from God's word, but at the same time he sees individuals formed by God's word. These are nurtured in righteousness and become people of God, fully complete. The Elijah-man is the man of God, prepared for his mission in the last times and for the coming of Jesus. Elijah is not a strange individualist, a being of some exceptional kind; but he is the archetype of the man of God, who will arise in the Bride-Church in the last days, the man who will be fully prepared for the coming of Jesus. How then shall I be, so as to be ready when Jesus comes? Study Elijah, and you will find the answer!

Elijah was ready for the final tasks

The man of God is to be complete, thoroughly equipped for every good work (2 Timothy 3:17). When Elijah was on Mount Horeb, he received his final orders. He was told to anoint two men to be kings, and to anoint Elisha to be a prophet in his place (1 Kings 19:15–16). When the day came when Elijah was about to be taken up to heaven, he knew that he should first go to Bethel, as there was something he had to do there; then after that, he had to go with the Lord's message to Jericho. Then he was ready; he had fully carried out all his appointed tasks (2 Kings 2:1–5). When the time came for his ascension, he had done all that the Lord had asked him to do, and also all that he himself had wanted to do.

Paul, the man of God, had a similar experience. At the end of his life he could say, *'I have finished the race'* (2 Timothy 4:7). Earlier, at Ephesus, Paul knew that at that time he had not yet finished his race (Acts 20:24).

The Lord leads people into spiritual maturity so that they can carry out his very special assignments on earth. In the last times, he will bring many people of God to maturity, so that they can make the final preparations for the coming of the King. That is part of the Elijah-ministry – to be one who prepares the way for the Lord (Malachi 3:1; Mark 1:2).

Elijah was a man of God even though he was not perfect

When Elijah was on Mount Horeb, a number of things occurred in his spiritual development. He had fled from Jezebel, who threatened his life. At Horeb, he received the courage to return. The Lord gave him the victory over his tendency to run away. He had wished for his own death (1 Kings 19:4). We injure our deepest selves by wishing ourselves dead. The Lord revealed his glory through his gentle whisper, so as to do a miracle of inner healing in Elijah – a healing from those dark thoughts of death which had injured his hopes. Until Horeb, Elijah had been alone, and he had sat alone by the Kerith ravine. *'I am the only one left, and now they are trying to kill me too'*, (1 Kings 19:14), was Elijah's description of his situation. This description was not true in God's light. There were still seven thousand men left, whose knees had not bowed down to Baal (1 Kings 19:18). Elijah was told to anoint Elisha to succeed him as prophet, and he thereby acquired a disciple. A man of God needs also to be a man of fellowship; God has created man with a need for fellowship and not for solitariness. The Lord's gift of a disciple for Elijah was a way of perfecting Elijah; he got a disciple who never left him. Right to the end, Elisha stuck faithfully to his master; Elijah went straight into heaven, departing from that faithful relationship that the Lord had provided for his last days on earth.

When the Bible talks of men of God, it does not mean people who are perfect. It deals with people who by redemption through Christ have acquired a part of his life. Christ lives in them, and they have taken on a part of the divine nature. But it is people who allow themselves to develop spiritually who will go on to maturity.

Elijah – the man of God who is the friend of God

There is a further Kingdom sign seen in the restored man of God, something that we find also in Elijah. He was well informed of God's purposes. His own ascension did not come as a surprise to him (2 Kings 2). The companies of younger prophets informed him of it, but they did not need to do so; Elijah knew of it already. The Lord no longer calls us servants, but instead calls us friends (John 15:15). Friends are well informed of everything that Jesus hears from the Father. His prophets receive information about the Lord's secret counsel (Amos 3:7). The restored man of God comes to live in a constant flow of prophetic information which keeps him well abreast of the signs of the times. For the Bride-Church, the return of Jesus will not come as a surprise. We shall know when the time is near (Luke 21:27–32). We have no promise in the Bible that we shall know the date and the exact time when Jesus will return, but we shall know when he is near and standing at the door. Elijah did not know the exact time for his departure into heaven, but he knew when it was near.

Elijah will come before the day of the Lord

Elijah will return before the great and dreadful day of the Lord (Malachi 4:5–6). I maintain that Elijah is the type of the man who comes as a counter-balance to the Antichrist-type – the man of lawlessness, the man of destruction (2 Thessalonians 2:3–4).

Elijah, as the restored man, is God's plan for your life. He is the person who will be ready for Jesus when he comes. He is the type of personality that is going to be needed for the final assignments of the Church in the present age. He comes forward with great boldness as the Lord's authorised representative. He loves to be close to God's throne; he stands before the throne. He prays with authority and he has assumed responsibility in prayer for his nation. He is keenly interested in everything to do with Israel, and prays for Israel's conversion and salvation. He serves the Lord with boldness in those gifts of grace that he has received. You can recognise the Elijah-man by his gifts of working miracles, prophecy, distinguishing between spirits. In fact, I see in the End Time an Elijah-Church, a Church that collectively manifests the same prophetic ministry as Elijah. But this Church must be built up of Elijah-people, of restored men and women of God.

Chapter 3

The Ministry of Restoration

Elijah has a ministry of restoring all things (Matthew 17:11).
Heaven must contain Jesus *'until the times of restitution of all
things.'* (Acts 3:19–21, KJV). Elijah will come before the great
and dreadful day of the Lord (Malachi 4:5–6).

These three scriptures together tell us that Elijah has a task
of preparing for the return of Jesus by restoring all things. The
times of restoration take place in preparation for his return,
but restoration requires an instrument, a restorer.

Satan perverts the right ways of the Lord

In order to understand the need for restoration, we must
understand what Satan is doing. Paul exposed the plans of the
evil one, which he is for ever seeking to carry out through
those that serve him.

> *'You are a child of the devil and an enemy of everything
> that is right! You are full of all kinds of deceit and trickery.
> Will you never stop perverting the right ways of the Lord?'*
> (Acts 13:10)

God has right ways from the outset. He has a right way for
each individual. We are made in God's image, but it is not
long before Satan perverts the image of God until it is unre-
cognisable. God had a right way for the family, but look how
Satan has managed to pervert what God originally had in mind
for the family.

Satan has also perverted God's right ways for the Church. It started out in good order on the day of Pentecost when the Church was founded. But in the letters to the seven churches in Asia Minor, in Revelation 2–3, only two of those churches meet with approval. In two others, Sardis and Laodicea, the evil one had succeeded particularly well in his process of perversion. Often a movement of spiritual awakening, started by God's initiative, loses its original vision and after 50 years becomes only a perverted version of what God planned at the beginning. This is where the Elijah ministry comes in. It makes a straight highway through rugged places (Isaiah 40:1–5). This prophetic word particularly applies to John the Baptist, who fulfilled an Elijah ministry. He made right ways by his impassioned call for repentance, before Jesus began his public ministry in his first coming. Now a new ministry is needed, that will fulfil Isaiah's prophecy of level, paved roads, when Jesus appears the second time. Restoration is making straight what is crooked, and bringing it back to accord with God's original plan.

Jesus' redemption and reconciliation through his death are the grounds for restoration. He died to give us back what we had lost through the Fall. He brings us back into the original blessings of paradise. The ultimate purpose of reconciliation is a restored mankind back in a restored paradise – the new Jerusalem in a new earth. Then we shall finally have got back everything we have lost. With the redeeming work of Jesus as foundation, the man or woman of God can enter into an Elijah ministry and with the Lord's authority can restore individuals, families, churches, Israel, and nations.

Dividing the plunder

Jesus' work of reconciliation is like an attack on an enemy who has filled his house with stolen goods. After he has been overcome, a celebration of victory begins, when everyone who has been robbed can have his property restored to him.

They rejoice before you, *as men rejoice when dividing the plunder* (Isaiah 9:2–4). He will divide the spoils with the strong (the many) (Isaiah 53:12). Both these prophecies concern Jesus' work of salvation.

Jesus has entered the strong man's house (Matthew 12:29). The strong man is Satan, and his house is the world, which is in his power. But Jesus has bound the strong man, so the plundering of his household goods can begin. They are all captured goods, which have been taken from us. Thus far Jesus has come; the work of restitution is in full swing! All stolen goods can be claimed back by description. Restoration is receiving back what has been stolen away.

The ministry of restoration is stepping out boldly and taking from the enemy that which he has robbed from God's people.

When David and his men came back to Ziklag, a gang of robbers had carried off their wives, children and household goods. But David found strength in the Lord, and pursued the gang, fought and beat them, and took back everything the gang had taken, including wives, children and goods. Nothing was missing (1 Samuel 30).

God's people have been plundered and looted, and are waiting for someone who can say to the enemy, with God's authority, 'Give back!' (Isaiah 42:22).

In the time of Elijah, God's people were plundered and looted by the prophets of Baal and by the spiritual decline caused by Jezebel and Ahab seducing the people of Israel into apostasy. But Elijah, with the Lord's boldness, attacks this formidable enemy. The decisive victory happens on Mount Carmel. As we study to follow Elijah in the ministry of restoration, so the Carmel experience is a decisive victory over the powers that have overcome and plundered God's people. We shall see in many areas how it was before Carmel, and how it became after Carmel, and demonstrate how Elijah came to restore all things.

The Restoration of the Family

In Malachi's prophecy about the coming of Elijah in the End Time, it says that Elijah has a ministry of turning the fathers' hearts to the children, and the children's hearts to the fathers (Malachi 4:5–6).

On Mount Carmel, Elijah turned the hearts of the generations toward one another. The apostasy of the people had alienated them from the faith of the earlier generations in their God. The generation who lived in Elijah's time turned back in their hearts to Israel's first generation, Abraham, Isaac and Jacob. There is a flow of blessing between the generations. God has chosen to send his blessing by way of generations that are in harmony with one another. Before Isaac died, he wanted to bless his sons and grandsons (Genesis 49:1, 28). The blessing that Jacob gave to each of his sons was connected with that son's particular relationship with him. For example, Reuben had defiled his father's bed, and therefore the flow of blessing was held back (Genesis 49:3–4). Simeon and Levi had been guilty of violence and anger, so Jacob had to stay clear of their council, their company (5–7); but he could give his full blessing to Judah (8–10).

God is the source of the blessing; but the blessing flows between the generations when their hearts are open to one another. The blessing is a protection for the future for the younger generation.

> '*Honour your father and your mother, so that you may live long and that it may go well with you in your land.*'
>
> (Deuteronomy 5:16)

The older generation are to live in such a way that they have something from God to pass on to the younger, while the younger generation are to live in respect and obedience, in an attitude of willingness to receive a blessing from the older. But when the generation gap widens and their hearts are turned away from one another, then the flow of blessing ceases and the family are left without protection.

Elijah restored the flow of blessing between the generations. The channels that God has chosen for his blessing are the relationships between people. Blessings flow from older to younger, from parents to children. From Elizabeth, an older woman, to Mary, a younger one. From the teacher to his disciples. From Elijah to Elisha. From the leader to his followers. From Moses to Joshua. From a commander to those for whom he is responsible. Satan is out to destroy these channels of God's blessing. He does this by creating rebellion, barriers, and separation in the relationships.

The family as a protection against stormy times to come

Malachi describes the Elijah ministry as a protection against a future catastrophe: *'Or else I will come and strike the land with a curse'* (Malachi 4:6). If the family relationships are healed, the family can be a place of shelter, of protection against God's wrath. The unprotected family, whose hearts are turned away from one another, can be struck with a curse when a time of wrath comes. Healed relationships are an investment and a protection for the future.

What rooms shall we find to hide in, when God's wrath spreads over the earth? (Isaiah 26:20–21). When Israel was delivered from Egypt, the 'rooms' were the families, the households, who were under the protection of the blood (Exodus 12:1–4, 7, 15). Each family head was responsible for taking a lamb without defect for his family, slaughtering it and putting some of its blood on the sides and top of the door-frame of the house. The father has a priestly responsibility for his family. His fulfilment of this office is an important part of the protection we need during the difficult times that precede the coming of Jesus. The house had to be searched to be sure there was no yeast left in it. The New Testament application of this command to a family is that we are to clear out the yeast of malice and wickedness, so that sincerity and truth reign in the home (1 Corinthians 5:8). No part of the lamb was to be taken to another household; it was to be a protection for the family unit. The homes in Egypt thus shielded under the blood were protected from the destroying angel, because that was the divine ordering.

God's wrath arises against rebellion and chaos, such as prevails in the kingdom of darkness. The Kingdom of God is a kingdom of order, an order that finds its expression in the building-up of the home in accordance with the instructions in God's word. A household divided against itself will not stand (Matthew 12:25).

The king and his family in the time of Elijah

The king of Israel and his family in Elijah's time had abandoned the divine order. In effect, Ahab looked after affairs of
state, but handed over responsibility for religious matters to
his wife Jezebel. Ahab did not assume his proper responsibility as a priest in his family, and therefore he left an opening
for the destructive forces. Ahab sold himself to do what was
evil, when his wife Jezebel urged him to do so (1 Kings 21:25).
Jezebel enticed him into the worship of false gods (16:31). The
prophets of Baal sat at Jezebel's table. She was the one who
took the initiative in the field of religion.

There is a parallel here with the serpent's stratagem in the
garden of Eden when, through Eve, he drew Adam into sin.
Through Jezebel, Ahab was drawn into sin worse than any
other king before him. He refused to take his spiritual
responsibility for his wife and his family, and therefore the
family were left unprotected from the attacks of the enemy.

In the game of intrigue concerning the vineyard of Naboth
the Jezreelite, we get an insight into Ahab's family life. When
Ahab does not get his own way in his desire for Naboth's
vineyard, he lies on his bed sulking and refuses to eat. Jezebel
wonders why he is out of sorts. *'Is this how you act as king over
Israel? Get up and eat! Cheer up. I'll get you the vineyard of
Naboth the Jezreelite.'* Jezebel takes the initiative in the
economic crime that leads also to a murder. She herself writes
the letters giving instructions to put the plot into effect; she
writes them in the king's name and places his seal on them,
using his signet-ring. She also takes the initiative as soon as she
hears that Naboth is dead, and urges Ahab to go and take
possession of the stolen property. When Ahab arrives at the
vineyard, he meets the prophet Elijah, who pronounces judgment over Ahab, but more particularly over Jezebel (1 Kings
21:1–29).

This insight into Ahab's family life shows the man, sulky
and paralysed into inaction, and the liberated woman, taking
command of the family and the kingdom. But the picture also
shows the family as completely unprotected, the family that
the Lord strikes with a curse. The man has not taken the

responsibility given to him by the Lord, and the woman has rebelled against God's order for the home.

Satan abandoned the position that was his, in subjection under God's throne. Jezebel is the picture of the woman who has rebelled and abandoned the position that God has given to her in the family, in subjection to her husband. The restoration of the family means bringing the family back into God's order.

> *'Now I want you to realise that the head of every man is Christ, and the head of the woman is the man, and the head of Christ is God.'* (1 Corinthians 11:3)

That the man is the head of the woman does not mean that the man has any right to be a tyrant over the woman; it means that the man is the woman's protector. That Christ is the head of the Church means that Christ is the Church's protector and defender. We have never interpreted it as meaning that Christ should be a tyrant over the Church; his love makes that impossible.

To be the head means to take responsibility for leadership, and this is where the protection lies. Paul wanted men to lift up holy hands, without anger or disputing (1 Timothy 2:8). Hands are lifted, in the Bible, in order to bless. You who are the father of a family, you have a calling to be an intercessor for your wife and your children. When did you last have a day of prayer and fasting for your family? Your intercession forms a protection for your family when the time of wrath comes.

What did Elijah do for the family?

What had Malachi seen as a prophetic clue in the life of Elijah, that led him to believe that the Elijah ministry in the End Time was bound up with the restoration of the family? The Jews took the actions in Elijah's life and read into them prophetic models or precedents. Elijah lived during the time of drought at the home of the widow of Zarephath. Then it happened that the widow's son became ill, and finally stopped breathing. The widow said to Elijah, *'What do you have*

*against me, man of God? Did you come to remind me of my sin
and kill my son?'* (1 Kings 17:17–18). In some way the widow's
conscience was struck with the thought that her own sin was
the cause of God's judgment on her son. The presence of the
man of God in her home had awakened to life some guilt from
the past. *'Give me your son!'* said Elijah, and taking the child
from her arms, he carried him to the upper room where he was
staying. There he began to call upon God, as a mediator for
the woman, to turn aside God's wrath from the boy. *'O Lord
my God, have you brought tragedy also upon this widow I am
staying with, by causing her son to die?'* It is true that the Lord
visits the sins of the fathers upon the children. When Elijah
calls upon God, he seeks to turn aside that visitation from the
child. The Lord heard Elijah's cry, and the boy's life returned
to him, and he lived. Then Elijah was able to give the boy back
to his mother with the word, *'Look, your son is alive!'* Perhaps
Malachi was inspired by this scene of restoration. Elijah turns
the widow to the son in her joy, and the son to his mother, and
they find one another again in a joyful close relationship.

This child of death, restored to life, is a picture of the youth
of the last generation, suffering under the sin of the fathers,
under threat of death from nuclear weapons and also from all
the other evil powers that have been released: pornography,
video violence, drugs, AIDS. In Psalm 102:16–20, the coming
generation are called those condemned to death, literally *'children of death'*. But through the Elijah ministry, a lost generation can be brought back to life in God, the generation gaps
can be bridged, God's wrath can be turned aside, and the
younger generation can become the last great harvest of this
age.

The restoration of the family lay in what happened at Carmel. There, Elijah put right man's relationship with God. The
people recognised the Lord as God, and renounced at the
same time the worship of false gods. When our relationship
with God is broken, it has a negative effect on our other
relationships. The permissiveness in the last days has an effect
on the family. People will be disobedient to their parents,
without love, unforgiving; but an explanation of this break-up

of the family lies in the statement that they will also be godless (2 Timothy 3:1–3). When the people were gathered on Mount Carmel, they very likely stood together by families. Every one of them was brought into a right relationship with God. In chorus, they confessed: *'The Lord – he is God!'* In this confession, they also found one another. When they opened their hearts to God, they also opened their hearts to one another.

On Carmel, too, Elijah did battle against the Asherah cult, the fertility goddess who was worshipped in sex orgies. The Asherah cult broke down family trust and loyalty in the same way that pornography has broken down the morals of the western world. When Elijah rid the land of 400 prophets of Asherah, it had the same kind of effect that there would have been in Sweden if all the porn-films and men's magazines were swept away in a single day. Elijah battled against the powers that were breaking down families in Israel.

Those groups who work for the take-over of society by the forces of Antichrist, try systematically to break down marriage, to free pornography from any restraint, to spread propaganda in favour of cohabitation without marriage, to bring in the homosexual life-style and make it acceptable, to organise economic discrimination against marriage so that it will no longer be attractive, to drive the women out to earn so as to split families and foment war between the sexes. The Antichrist would not be able to achieve his purpose of world domination without these forward troops of lawlessness who have established the range for the enemy guns to destroy the family. Against this background, the Elijah ministry is needed to restore the family.

The angel Gabriel used the same prophetic word about John the Baptist as Malachi used concerning the Elijah ministry. Compare Luke 1:17 with Malachi 4:5–6! John the Baptist would turn the hearts of the fathers to their children and so make ready a people prepared for the Lord. From this we can draw the following conclusion in the face of Jesus' second coming: it is in families that we prepare ourselves for his coming, and it is restored families that are ready for that coming.

The delivery of the children of Israel from Egypt can be compared to the redemption of the church at the coming of Jesus. The children of Israel were delivered by families. The Lord wanted to save Lot's family, but that was not completely achieved. The Lord delivered Noah's family, eight persons, from a catastrophic judgment. Both these events are used as prototype illustrations of the coming of Jesus. Deliverance in the last days, too, will have family unity as its starting point.

The Restoration of the Church

In Old Testament times there was a prophetic movement. Before Elijah's public appearance, this prophetic movement had been silenced and frightened underground through violent persecution. Elijah poured out his heart before the Lord, and described the spiritual situation:

> *'The Israelites have rejected your covenant, broken down your altars, and put your prophets to death with the sword. I am the only one left.'* (1 Kings 19:14)

In the persecution, prophets had been killed with the sword. The prophets of Baal and of Asherah had become the official leadership recognised by the state. They were false prophets, leading the people astray.

One of Ahab's courtiers, Obadiah, worshipped God zealously, but did not dare to raise his voice against Ahab's apostasy. He had taken a hundred prophets and hidden them away in two caves, fifty in each, and had supplied them with food and water (1 Kings 18:3–4). The prophetic movement in Elijah's time needed to be freed from fear. Elijah's ministry freed the people of God from fear and gave them freedom to act in Israel. After Elijah's departure, Elisha was able to have a school of prophets, and even before Elijah's ascension there were groups of prophets at Bethel and Jericho. Those who had previously stayed hidden in caves were now able to live in freedom.

If we compare the courtier Obadiah, who was frightened

into silence for fear of Ahab and Jezebel, with Elisha's servant Gehazi, who was on a visit to the king and openly told him of the miracles that Elisha was doing in support of his request to the king, then we realise what a great change had come over the people of God in Israel (2 Kings 8:4–5).

When the Lord restores his people, he gives them leaders

During the decline before the coming of Elijah, there was no spiritual leadership capable of raising its voice against the prophets of Baal. Through Elijah, God gave back to Israel a prophetic leadership, which continued when Elijah anointed Elisha to succeed him.

A restored fellowship

Elijah was at first a lone prophet, but after the Lord met with him at Horeb, he came into fellowship with Elisha. The Church today is restored through the relationships that arise through fellowship.

The church is restored through training of disciples

In the process of restoration, it was arranged that Elijah acquired a disciple in Elisha. Elisha in turn took many disciples through his school of prophets. So that which Elijah handed on to Elisha during his period of instruction became multiplied many times at the next stage.

The Restoration of the Nation

At the time of Elijah's arrival on the public scene, Israel was divided into two nations, Judah and Israel. This division was a punishment, because Solomon had turned away from God and had become a worshipper of false gods (1 Kings 11:9–13). When Elijah builds up the altar of the Lord which lies in ruins on Mount Carmel, he makes a striking confession of national unity. He takes twelve stones to build the altar, one for each of the twelve tribes of Israel. Elijah understood that the division between God's people was a curse, which was preventing the revelation of God's glory. When God cannot use the voices of men, he uses stones. The twelve stones were an announcement, made in faith, of the unity between God's people. The altar was finished by the time of the evening sacrifice. From this altar, reconciliation was brought to Israel, and it was there that God's glory was revealed (1 Kings 18:30–32).

It is noteworthy to compare how the relationship between Judah and Israel stood before the Mount Carmel confrontation with the way it stood after it.

Before Carmel

The kings in both lands were at war with one anther as long as they lived. This applied first to Rehoboam and Jeroboam (1 Kings 15:6–7). Then there was war between Abijah and Jeroboam. Then came two kings, Asa and Baasha, and they too remained at war with one another throughout their reigns (15:16). During Omri's time, Israel itself was further split into two factions (16:21). The period before Elijah was thus a story of strife and division.

After Carmel

The king of Israel asked Jehoshaphat, king of Judah, if he would go with him against a common enemy. Jehoshaphat answered the king of Israel,

> *'I am as you are, my people as your people, my horses as your horses!'*   (1 Kings 22:1–4)

Joram and Jehoshaphat could work together in a similar way (2 Kings 3:7). There was a new atmosphere of unity and cooperation after Elijah made his declaration of unity.

On two occasions in my own experience, we have made such declarations of unity by building an Elijah-altar, during Christian meetings. On one of these occasions, we took representatives from various denominations. About ten persons from different denominations were represented in a service of intercession. After they had grasped one another's hands and declared their unity, they were able to serve in giving communion to God's people. On another occasion, when we were praying for unity in Sweden across political groupings and class barriers, we took one representative from each of the main political parties, also one farmer and one recent immigrant. They stood there hand in hand, and publicly confessed that they were one, with Christ as their head, and so represented symbolically what God's will was for our land.

Chapter 4

The Prophet with Responsibility for the Nation

Elijah – the prophet with responsibility for the nation

Elijah took on his shoulders the prophetic responsibility for his people and his nation, which led him to be an intercessor for the nation (James 5:17–18; 2 Chronicles 7:14). He did battle against the nation's spiritual enemies; he understood, in his spirit, the people's spiritual condition. He was a watchman, sounding the alarm to warn of the dangers (Ezekiel 33:7–9). At Carmel he was a guide for the people; he called them to restoration and recovery, and delivered them from destruction.

He was like a whole defending army for the nation. *'My father! My father! The chariots and horsemen of Israel!'*, Elisha cried out as he saw Elijah carried up to heaven (2 Kings 2:12).

Elijah was God's spokesman, a man who could say to the people and their leaders 'Thus says the Lord'. He brought guidance, warning and judgment to the kings. If he could not reach them in person, he wrote a letter or sent a message to them. He deposed and appointed kings, and pronounced judgments on them.

On Mount Horeb he was given the task of going and anointing two men to be kings (1 Kings 19:15–17). These two were then called upon to execute judgment against the house of Jezebel and Ahab.

Elijah lived in accordance with that which is also the

Church's responsibility – to pray for kings and all those in authority (1 Timothy 2:1–4).

The borders of the nations and our areas of responsibility

Is it right that we in our time should take responsibility for a nation as Elijah did? National feeling is out of fashion, particularly among some of the nations of Europe. Some talk with scorn of 'provincial attitudes'. It is more honourable to think internationally, as a world citizen. Nations are over-emphasised, many think; we ought to work for world peace, a global economy and the New World Order.

A world government without Christ would be a wild beast with all the accumulated 'beast' characteristics of earlier dictators. It would lead the world astray into chaos and destruction. God has set national boundaries as a protection against the world community of the Antichrist. God has created the peoples and has established the frontiers of the nations, so that people shall seek God within their borders (Acts 17:26–27).

The building of the tower of Babel was the first instance of men seeking a world kingdom, built with man's power and strength, where God's were excluded. To prevent this world kingdom of Antichrist from being started, God gave the people different languages and spread them out over the world (Genesis 11:1–9). God's division of the earth's inhabitants into nations with definite boundaries in this way is a protection against a world government without God.

In general, I believe that our national boundaries are a protection against the Antichrist, and should stay as they are until Jesus comes.

Jesus gave us, in the 'great commission', the responsibility to go and make disciples of *'all nations'* (Matthew 28:18). When Christ comes again, he will judge the *'nations'* (Matthew 25:32). When we give account before God, we do it both as individuals and as nations.

In the last times, people will be faithless and treacherous. Faithlessness is directed against the family and the nation, and will come to be, in particular, an economic treachery whereby the leaders of nations sell the nation's interests to multinational banks and businesses, which are working towards a power take-over by the Antichrist.

The Elijah ministry, God's people with national responsibility, will be a protection against this economic treachery. The Lord is calling at this time for intercessors for our countries who in faith, before Christ, will take responsibility for their countries.

'Or else I will come and strike the land with a curse'

Elijah is sent to put right family relationships, so that the Lord will not strike the land with a curse (Malachi 4:5–6). This curse is the complete annihilation of people and of their property, like that which struck Sodom and Gomorrah. There, because of the homosexual life-style of the people, the Lord struck the whole area with a curse. The same judgment struck Jericho; because of it no-one was allowed to save anything from the city when it came under God's wrath. Both people and their belongings were completely destroyed (Joshua 7:10–13; 6:16–18).

When Elijah rebuilt the ruined altar on Carmel, he restored the people's respect for a holy God, and turned aside the wrath of God directed against Israel. Elijah knew that Ahab had done more to provoke God's wrath than anyone else before him (1 Kings 16:30–33). The altar was in ruins, signifying that no sacrifice for sin had been offered on behalf of Israel. God's anger was a constant threat of judgment to them.

Elijah built up the altar and sacrificed a bull as a sin-offering to turn aside God's wrath. When he prayed for fire, he knew that God's holiness is like a consuming fire. If he had not brought reconciliation for the people through the sacrifice, there would have been no one left on Mount Carmel when he finished his prayer and opened his eyes. The people would all have been struck with a curse. The fire that fell on Carmel was not merely a harmless revelation of God's glory. The fire could both create joy among the people, because it showed them the glory of God, and could also put to death those who were under God's judgment. This had happened before in the history of Israel (Leviticus 9:22–24; 10:1–3).

Turning aside God's wrath

Elijah's task was to stand in the way of God's wrath and to
turn it aside from striking the people. He was a mediator
between the people and God. Anyone who takes on the Elijah
ministry must understand the wrath of God, something that
people find it hard to grasp these days, as God's holiness has
been erased from their picture of him. When God pronounces
a judgment of annihilation, he is being utterly righteous. God
was righteous when he condemned Sodom and Gomorrah to
destruction. The End Time is called the time of wrath, because
God has withheld his wrath until an appointed time, when his
judgment will strike the earth, which by then will have filled
up the full measure of its sin. But there is at all times a space
left for intercessors to come forward and turn God's wrath
aside.

The man whom God seeks, who will come forward and
stand in the gap on behalf of the land, has as his most important task the turning aside of God's wrath.

> *'I looked for a man among them who would build up the
> wall and stand before me in the gap on behalf of the land so
> that I would not have to destroy it, but I found none. So I
> will pour out my wrath upon them and consume them with
> my fiery anger, bringing down on their own heads all they
> have done, declares the Sovereign Lord.'*
>
> (Ezekiel 22:30–31)

In Elijah, the Lord found a man who could turn aside his
wrath.

How can we possibly pray for the turning aside of God's
wrath from a whole people? Daniel was able to pray in this
way, by identifying himself with the whole people, sharing
their burden of sin and confessing it as his own, standing as the
people's representative in prayer before God. He prayed that
God's wrath and curse should be turned aside, and continued
until God's countenance once again shone over the devastated
sanctuary, until he was assured that God had granted forgive-
ness (Daniel 9). Through his intercession he turned the course
of history from punishment to restoration.

If Sodom had had ten righteous men in it who had stood in the way of God's wrath, God would have spared the town. Someone has worked out that the total population of Sodom and all the towns destroyed with it would have been 100,000. Each of the ten righteous men would then have been representing 10,000 people. So each intercessor who prays for his country can be thought of as praying for 10,000 persons, bringing their case before God.

Elijah-ministry to Israel

Elijah will deliver Israel in the last days from wholesale destruction, and turn its people to the Messiah. Israel will come to its moment of great need when all other nations of the world turn against her and are ready to annihilate her. The most serious aspect is that these other nations and their armies are only instruments for the carrying out of God's wrath and punishment. Israel has gone into the land without the protection of the blood. No sacrifice has covered their sins, and they have not felt any need to be reconciled to God. But Elijah will show them the way of salvation from destruction; he will point to the Lamb of God, who takes away the sins of the world. The sacrificial lamb, who delivered them from the angel of death and destruction in Egypt, has appeared in human form in the Messiah, and they will look to him, the one they have pierced, and confess him as Lord and Saviour. This will bring their deliverance from destruction.

Praising the Lord for his acts of judgment

God wants his people to understand his holiness in such a deep way that they can praise him for his acts of judgment in the End Time. Before the angels come forward with the bowls of his wrath, which will be poured out over the earth, the song of Moses and of the Lamb will be sung, a song of praise to God for his righteousness displayed in his acts. We will all shout 'Hallelujah!' when the judgment against the great prostitute is executed, she who corrupted the earth by her adulteries.

> *'After this I heard what sounded like the roar of a great multitude in heaven shouting: "Hallelujah! Salvation and glory and power belong to our God, for true and just are his judgments. He has condemned the great prostitute who corrupted the earth by her adulteries. He has avenged on her the blood of his servants."'*   (Revelation 19:1–2).

It does not belong only to the spirit of the Old Testament to praise the Lord for his righteous acts of judgment; that spirit will be one with that of the Church in the End Time in praising the Lord for his judgments of wrath. His people will urge him to execute his judgment on the great prostitute.

> *'Give back to her as she has given; pay her back double for what she has done. Mix her a double portion from her own cup. Give her as much torture and grief as the glory and luxury she gave herself.'*   (Revelation 18:6–7)

Elijah, who turned God's wrath aside from the people, could also be at one with God's wrath against the prophets of Baal and Jezebel, the seducers of the people in that time.

When Jesus comes and reveals the wrath of the Lamb, he is surprised that no one helps him, that there is nobody among the people who gives him support. They ask him:

> *'Why are your garments red, like those of one treading the winepress?'* *'I have trodden the winepress alone; from the nations no one was with me. I trampled them in my anger.'*   (Isaiah 63:1–6)

We have too much of a sickly-sweet picture of 'gentle Jesus meek and mild', so that we have difficulty in recognising Jesus again when he comes covered in blood. Because we do not recognise him, he gets no help with the execution of his terrible task. When the year of his salvation comes, he must turn his wrath upon the oppressors and the seducers. For them, the year of jubilee is a year of revenge.

We have, too, in our Western countries persons who

exercise the ministry of the prophets of Baal by leading people astray in lawlessness, occultism, dissolution of the home, homosexuality. When they have filled up the measure of their sins, we shall join in praying that the Lamb in his wrath will put a stop to their false leading, so that Jesus will no longer stand alone in carrying out his mission.

Elijah's Task – Standing in the Way

When Ahab's and Jezebel's whole conspiracy against Naboth had been carried through, when Naboth had been murdered and Ahab was on his way to take possession of Naboth's vineyard, the Lord's command came to Elijah:

> *'Go down to meet Ahab king of Israel, who rules in Samaria. He is now in Naboth's vineyard, where he has gone to take possession of it. Say to him, "This is what the Lord says: Have you not murdered a man and seized his property?" Then say to him, "This is what the Lord says: In the place where dogs licked up Naboth's blood, dogs will lick up your blood – yes, yours!"'*
>
> (1 Kings 21:17–19)

Elijah stood in the way of the economic crime that was being committed in the highest quarters, in the royal family of Israel. He stood so directly in the way, that he arrived to meet Ahab at the exact psychological moment, sent there by the Lord to awaken Ahab's conscience. It was a compliment in God's eyes that Ahab called Elijah *'My enemy'*, because he truly was an enemy of the lawlessness that Ahab represented. Elijah pronounced sentence on Ahab, though their meeting ended with Ahab humbling himself, so that the Lord postponed execution of his sentence (27–29).

Elijah stood in the way of occultism

Ahab's son and successor, King Ahaziah, injured himself and was seriously ill. So he sent a message to Baal-Zebub, the god of Ekron, an occult oracle, to find out whether he would recover (2 Kings 1:2–3).

> *'But the angel of the Lord said to Elijah the Tishbite, "Go up and meet the messengers of the king of Samaria and ask them, 'Is it because there is no God in Israel that you are going off to consult Baal-Zebub, the god of Ekron?' Therefore this is what the Lord says: 'You will not leave the bed you are lying on. You will certainly die!'"'*

Elijah went. He stood in the way of the king's messengers and sent them back to the king with their errand unaccomplished.

Can the prophetic Church stand silently by in passive acceptance while economic crime increases and the occult wave surges over our countries? We shall, like Elijah, stubbornly resist, and by every possible means we shall stand in the way of the lawlessness spreading out over our lands. Up until recently, the conspiracy of lawlessness, which has caused the de-Christianising of our Western culture, has been able to work freely, undisturbed by stubborn Elijah-people.

Stopping the man of lawlessness

Paul had previously told the church at Thessalonica of something that was holding back the man of lawlessness and preventing him from being revealed before his proper time (2 Thessalonians 2:6). We do not know what it was that restrained him, and can only guess at it. But if we compare the prophetic pattern shown in Elijah, we can see the prophet who stood in the way of lawlessness.

Satan's strategy for taking control over the world through Antichrist is to break down man's respect for the ten commandments and everything else that is holy, so that he can take them captive by means of occult delusions. In Sweden, we have already seen this strategy being worked out step by step in the plan for the Antichrist's power take-over. First came the wave of pornography, with its propaganda in favour of pre-marital sexual relationships, unfaithfulness, and cohabitation without marriage. The man who breaks the commandment by committing adultery, then probably lies to his wife; in this way his conscience is already seared. The next step is that he is dishonest at work. Shady transactions, tax fiddling, stealing from his employer, and economic crime are only the next steps for someone who has already set out on the road of lawlessness. Those who refuse to love the truth come under the judgment of God:

> *'For this reason God sends them a powerful delusion so that they will believe the lie and so that all will be condemned who have not believed the truth but have delighted in wickedness.'*　　　　(2 Thessalonians 2:11–12)

The delusions and the occult wave have been the forward troops of the Antichrist, but they would not have succeeded in drawing so many followers among the Swedish people, if there had not already been manipulation of men's minds to abandon the ten commandments.

According to the book of Revelation, lawlessness in the last times specially implies murder, magic arts, sexual immorality and thefts (Revelation 9:21). In spite of all wars, the greatest number of killings occur through the many millions of abortions each year throughout the world. Unfaithfulness between spouses and crooked business dealings are on the increase, and occult practices and witchcraft are spreading among those who have abandoned God's commands. Lawlessness has also infiltrated parts of the Church and silenced its capability to resist. But the prophetic Church, exercising an Elijah ministry, will be a constant irritation to the conspiracy of lawlessness, and will keep its foot on the brake until the last day of this age.

Many Christians have become so adapted to, and influenced by, liberal thinking that they believe it wrong to make a stand against the spread of lawlessness. But let us, like Elijah, stand in the strategic positions where the Lord has posted us by his commands, in order to be a plague on all those making plans for the overthrow of our countries by the Antichrist!

How long will we waver between two opinions?

When the people of Israel and all the prophets of Baal had assembled on Mount Carmel, Elijah went before the people and challenged their attitude of neutrality: *'How long will you waver between two opinions?'* (1 Kings 18:21). They had in their ideology found a method of co-existence between God and Baal, which affected their thinking accordingly. But how did it look in practice? Co-existence was impossible. Elijah's was the last voice to be raised before a total dictatorship would have taken over. The prophets had been killed, and the prophets of Baal were permanent party-guests at the court. The whole people had bowed the knee before Baal and had given Baal their kiss of greeting – their loyalty. There were only 7,000 left who had not given way to the prevailing tyranny. What had cleared the way for this religious dictatorship was the politics of neutrality.

It is difficult for us to realise that in the kingdom of Antichrist there will be such a dictatorship that only those who bear the mark of the beast will be able to buy and sell, and that all who do not, will be under the threat of beheading. How can such a dictatorship sneak into place? It can indeed, if we choose to remain neutral in the face of all the delusions and destructive powers in the community; neutral, with the motive of giving freedom of expression to all opinions.

Our experience in Sweden is that it is exactly this way of thinking that is causing the de-Christianising of our country. In 1969, the then Minister of Justice launched the 'politics of neutrality' in the area of family law reform. In his directive to the family law experts, he said: 'New legislation should as far as possible be neutral in relation to different forms of living together and moral conceptions'. The Minister wanted in this way to abolish the wedding as the legal basis for marriage, so that it would be sufficient just to register at, say, a local social insurance office. This type of directive has become customary in the case of all legislation concerning family life since 1969, with the result that our laws have become neutral as between (1) marriage and (2) cohabitation without marriage; and between (1) marriage between man and woman and (2) homosexuals living together. But the morally destructive powers opposing marriage have not been neutral in their intention to take control over Sweden. Under the cloak of neutrality they are slowly working towards the abolition of marriage. Under this cloak, too, Sweden is in the process of being taken over by foreign religions. Christianity as an educational subject is of course abolished, and replaced by a neutral religious instruction that is neutral as between various views about life. This is the ideology of neutrality, which has been a curse upon Sweden and has destroyed morals and de-Christianised our country. Where are the Elijah voices that will challenge and expose this 'politics of neutrality' so honoured in the eyes of Swedish people?

Chapter 5

Sorcerers and Magicians

Elijah had both a love and a responsibility for the Jewish people. They had, however, been led astray by false leaders, 450 prophets of Baal and 400 prophets of Asherah, Jews who had sold themselves to Satan, who were involved in magic and sorcery, and worshipped false gods.

Baal was a god who was invoked for welfare, fertility and success. Asherah or Astarte was a mother-goddess, worshipped either as a goddess of war or else as a sun or moon goddess. As a mother-goddess, she is often depicted with a child in her arms, with some resemblances to pictures of the Madonna.

The prophets of Baal had both religious and political power in the time of Elijah. They were standing guests at the royal court, thanks to their contacts with Jezebel. It was a power group comprising the magicians, the king's family, and Satan.

Satan has a particular interest in getting control over Jews who have sold themselves to him. He is well aware of God's plan for the kingdom of peace, and of the key role of the house of David in the fulfilment of the promises. Satan needs the Jews in order to reach his goal of world domination; he tries to gain control of nations by means of Jewish magicians, and we can imagine that through such people the Antichrist will come to power.

King Solomon was led astray by his many wives into becoming a worshipper of false gods. The satanic 'churches' look on Solomon as the first satanic worshipper, and derive much of their knowledge from Solomon's secret wisdom (1 Kings 11:1–13).

One of the kings of Judah who fell deepest into the worship of other gods was Manasseh.

> '*In both courts of the temple of the Lord, he built altars to all the starry hosts. He sacrificed his sons in the fire in the valley of Ben Hinnom, practised sorcery, divination and witchcraft, and consulted mediums and spiritists. He did much evil in the eyes of the Lord, provoking him to anger.*'
>
> (2 Chronicles 33:5–6)

Manasseh led Judah and the people of Jerusalem so far astray that they did more evil than the peoples that the Lord had driven out of the land of Canaan so that Israel could possess it.

The Jewish magician Bar-Jesus

In Acts, we are given a striking instance of the way in which a Jewish magician could have power over a Roman governor. This was discovered when Paul came to Paphos in Cyprus, and sought to preach the Gospel to Sergius Paulus, the Roman governor. The Jewish magician was much in favour with the governor and had a strong influence over him. He tried to stop him from receiving Christ, but Paul unmasked the magician, saying:

> '*You are a child of the devil and an enemy of everything that is right! You are full of all kinds of deceit and trickery. Will you never stop perverting the right ways of the Lord?*'

The Lord struck the magician with blindness, and Sergius Paulus was freed from his influence and came to faith in Jesus (Acts 13:6–12).

Simon the sorcerer of Samaria

In Samaria there was a man named Simon, who practised sorcery and had amazed the people of Samaria.

> *'He boasted that he was someone great, and all the people, both high and low, gave him their attention and exclaimed, "This man is the divine power known as the Great Power." They followed him because he had amazed them for a long time with his magic.'* (Acts 8:9–11)

A magician has a great influence over a neighbourhood because of his knowledge of black magic. Simon tried to worm his way into the Church of Christ. In him were combined the forces of finance and witchcraft, the same combination that the Church is going to encounter in the last times in the merchants, who are the world's great men, and in those who lead all the nations astray by their magic (Revelation 18:23).

The Elijah ministry in confrontation with Jewish magic

All the various combining forces will be in place when Elijah comes forward in the last times. The confrontation with the prophets of Baal is going to be repeated on a larger scale with Jewish sorcerers and magicians.

There are several Old Testament prophecies that describe the transition to the kingdom of the Messiah as the final reckoning with the idolatry of Israel. Read, for example, Isaiah 2! First, Isaiah prophesies about an everlasting peace on earth, and then he speaks of the final reckoning with the worship of false gods, when men will flee to caves in the rocks to hide from the presence of the Lord.

> *'You have abandoned your people, the house of Jacob. They are full of superstitions from the East; they practise divination like the Philistines, and clasp hands with pagans ... there is no end to their treasures.'* (Isaiah 2:6–7)

Isaiah is prophesying that the Jews will clasp hands with pagans in order to become rich, and that this alliance is founded on superstitions from the East. Zechariah 13:1–2 says that when the fountain is opened for the cleansing of the inhabitants of Jerusalem, the Lord will banish the names of the idols from the land. Will the idols really follow Israel until the time of the Messiah comes in and Israel are restored? Read Ezekiel 11:17–21; Zephaniah 1:4–7; Isaiah 66!

The time of reckoning with the false shepherds of Israel

When the good shepherd of Israel comes, he will rebuke the false shepherds, who have only taken care of themselves and made themselves rich, instead of taking care of the flock (Ezekiel 34). The Lord's anger burns against the shepherds, because they deal with false gods, soothsaying, false dreams, and give comfort in vain (Zechariah 10:1–3).

The prophets give us a strong warning that Israel is under the influence of false leaders, leaders who have to do with magic, idolatry and Eastern superstition, right up to the time when Messiah comes. That is why a new Elijah is needed, a new Carmel, and a new reckoning with the Jewish magicians who have led the world astray.

Intercessors for Israel with a gift of discerning spirits

Christians' love for Israel should not be so romantic that they are blinded to the fact that Israel too can have false leaders. At the same time, our love for Israel must be so strong that if, some day, it becomes clear that Israel has had leaders who are Satan-worshippers and have deliberately led the world astray into lawlessness and into the realm of Antichrist, we shall not give way to anti-semitism. We shall love Israel as Elijah did, and as Jesus did. Jesus was the good shepherd for the people, but he strongly opposed the false leaders.

Ezekiel had a horrifying vision of what the elders of Israel were doing inside the temple. Through a hole in the wall, he saw men bowing down to the sun (Ezekiel 8:4–18). The elders of the house of Israel today are as capable of concealing their black magic as those of Ezekiel's time, but what has been done secretly in the dark will be proclaimed from the roofs (Luke 12:1–3).

It follows directly from the situation with the sins of the false leaders, that the Lord seeks intercessors who are willing to stand in the gap before the Lord and be responsible for the land.

> *'There is a conspiracy of her princes within her like a roaring lion tearing its prey; they devour people, take treasures and precious things and make many widows within her. Her priests do violence to my law and profane my holy things; they do not distinguish between the holy and the common; ... Her officials within her are like wolves tearing their prey; they shed blood and kill people to make unjust gain.'*
> (Ezekiel 22:25–27)

When Ezekiel saw this conspiracy between the princes (officials) and the false leaders, formed to make themselves rich and to encourage lawlessness, he heard the Lord's urgent call for intercessors.

In order that the wrath of the Lord does not completely wipe out Israel and the world, intercessors are needed who are awake to the intrigues aiming at a power take-over by the Antichrist, who can turn God's wrath aside from the people.

An intercessor must know what Israel's hardness of heart is – the intercessor for Israel has to pray away the darkness and the hardness, so that Israel can come into the light and recognise their Messiah. Paul said: *'Israel has experienced a hardening in part until the full number of the Gentiles has come in'* (Romans 11:25). These dark facts are caused by Israel being deluded by leaders who serve the rulers of the kingdom of darkness.

Sorcery of the prophets of Baal

The prophets of Baal, by means of their success in sorcery and magic, had managed to gain power over most of the people of Israel in the time of Elijah. There were only 7,000 men left who had not bowed down to Baal. All those who had given their allegiance to Baal must surely have benefited in some way from the connection. Baal was a god of welfare, and people prayed to him for good harvests, or for rain to fall at the right times, or for a reasonable income. They must have received some of these things when they bowed the knee to Baal. The covenant with Baal can be compared with the covenant for material well-being that people will have to enter into with the Antichrist, in order to have the right to buy and sell.

When Elijah prayed his prayer and said to Ahab that there would be no rain in the next few years except at his, Elijah's, word, he made the sorcery of the prophets of Baal powerless, and disarmed the demons who were behind Baal. Later, Elijah called the prophets of Baal together to a major challenge on Mount Carmel. The prophets of Baal were to have an altar and to perform their sorcery openly in front of all the people. It is not usually Satan's procedure to do such things out in the open in front of everyone. That which worked well enough in the dark did not work at all in the light of day. They danced round their altar slashing themselves with swords and spears, as was their custom, until the blood flowed. Most sorcerers need blood in order to be able to conjure up demonic powers, so the prophets of Baal made use of their own blood. They continued their frantic prophesying until the time for the evening sacrifice (1 Kings 18:23–29). Because he prayed, and because he came forward so boldly, Elijah caused the power of the prophets of Baal in sorcery and magic to come to nothing.

Worshipping Satan in order to gain power over the earth

The devil showed Jesus all the kingdoms of the world and offered him power over the earth if Jesus would fall down and worship him, but Jesus answered: *'It is written: Worship the Lord your God and serve him only'* (Luke 4:5–8). Satan has made similar offers to many others. We must never exclude from our minds that there are people on earth today who have accepted Satan's invitation and worship him, working resolutely for him in accordance with his instructions in order to gain that power over the whole world that he invites them to receive.

The prostitute and the merchants will take power over the earth by means of witchcraft.

> *'Your merchants were the world's great men. By your magic spell all the nations are led astray.'*
>
> (Revelation 18:23)

The Babylon community – a kingdom built on witchcraft

The judgment on Babylon is prophetically pronounced by Isaiah in Isaiah 47:1–15. There is a clear parallel between Revelation 18 and Isaiah 47. Compare Isaiah 47:8 with Revelation 18:7: *'I will never be a widow or suffer the loss of children.'*

Isaiah shows that the Babylon community is built up by means of many sorceries and potent spells (Isaiah 47:9). Therefore,

> *'Disaster will come upon you, and you will not know how to conjure it away.'*　　　　　　　　　　(Isaiah 47:11)

> *'Keep on then, with your magic spells and with your many sorceries, which you have laboured at since childhood. Perhaps you will succeed, perhaps you will cause terror. All the counsel you have received has only worn you out! Let your astrologers come forward, those star-gazers who make predictions month by month, let them save you from what is coming upon you.'*　　　　(Isaiah 47:12–13)

This counsel and these magic spells had been carefully concealed. *'You have trusted in your wickedness and have said, "No one sees me"'* (Isaiah 47:10).

Isaiah has given us an insight into how the anti-Christian society manages to make its conquests. It is through astrologers who cast horoscopes, through sorcery and consulting with spirits in secret meetings. But Isaiah shows us also that quite suddenly, the sorceries will cease to help any longeer, and ruin will come suddenly upon the last assumption of power by the Antichrist.

The prophet Ezekiel shows us how the king of Babylon made his conquests by the use of occult sorceries.

> *'For the king of Babylon will stop at the fork in the road, at the junction of the two roads, to seek an omen: He will cast lots with arrows, he will consult his idols, he will examine*

*the liver. Into his right hand will come the lot for
Jerusalem, where he is to set up battering-rams.'*

(Ezekiel 21:21–22)

In the prophecies of Nahum too, concerning the judgment
against Nineveh, there are parallels with the destruction of the
kingdom of Antichrist in Revelation 17–18.

*'Woe to the city of blood, full of lies, full of plunder, never
without victims! ... all because of the wanton lust of a
harlot, alluring, the mistress of sorceries, who enslaved
nations by her prostitution and peoples* (families) *by her
witchcraft.'*

(Nahum 3:1, 4)

It is quite conceivable that the kingdom of this world cap-
tures people by black magic, by handing the nations over to
evil powers. Family ties are broken by the holding of satanic
ceremonies; demonic spirits are conjured up to bring about
unfaithfulness in families, to lead young people into living
together without marriage, and young men into homosexual
relationships. Those who seek to conquer the world for Satan
prepare the way for their conquest by means of witchcraft.

Until recently it would perhaps have appeared unrealistic
and strange to think along these lines in a society that believes
in science and has given up believing in the supernatural. But
since the arrival of the wave of occultism, with occult leaders
laying claim to influencing governments, we must wake up and
take into account that God's word has not merely given us
metaphorical language in the Old Testament about Babylon
and Nineveh to help us in knowing what happens at the end of
the age, but has given us a prophetic word that is to be
interpreted literally.

Many of the world's leaders have contacts with occult movements. They ask spiritualists and astrologers for advice. We
were surprised to learn how President Reagan and President
Gorbachev held their summit meetings on the days when the
activities of the satanists were at their highest. It was discovered that Nancy Reagan was advised by an astrologer

about the most favourable days for her husband to hold meetings to discuss world affairs – the days of the full moon.

Some leaders of nations have accepted the offer from Maharishi Mahesh Yogi, shown in full-page advertisements in leading newspapers: 'Maharishi invites people and governments to raise the ability of the government to satisfy everyone and create a problem-free nation by his TM-Sidhi programme. In this way the government will do justice to its sovereign authority and the whole nation will enjoy perpetual peace, happiness and prosperity – Heaven on Earth.'

When the leaders of nations open themselves to the occult, the risk increases that they will seek to manipulate themselves into greater power through the use of the occult or black magic.

Balaam's and Balak's sorceries in Israel

Balak the king of Moab, and Balaam his prophet, went up on hills around the camp of the people of Israel, built altars there and offered animal sacrifices to the gods of Moab. Their intention was to conquer Israel for the demonic powers and to lead the people astray by using their sorcery. It is true that Balaam could speak nothing else but blessings upon Israel, but Balak was always there maintaining his evil intentions, and by some means he succeeded. We can read the result in Numbers 25:1–12:

> 'While Israel was staying in Shittim, the men began to indulge in sexual immorality with Moabite women, who invited them to the sacrifices to their gods.'

Balak led Israel astray into worshipping false gods by means of Moabite women. The men were seduced through sorcery into immorality and infidelity. Seduction into immorality through the use of black magic has been a feature of the black arts from the very beginning.

Peter warns of false prophets who use Balaam's methods of tempting people into immorality in this way (2 Peter 2:9–22).

*'They have left the straight way and wandered off to follow
the way of Balaam the son of Beor ... for they mouth
empty, boastful words and, by appealing to the lustful
desires of sinful human nature, they entice people who are
just escaping from those who live in error.'*

(2 Peter 2:15; 18)

We need to penetrate and uncover Satan's strategy in order
that we can pray effectively. It is also a part of prophetic
vigilance to understand the games being played behind the
scenes, whereby the people of the earth are seduced.

The prostitute in Revelation 17–18 works through her sorcery to lead mankind into immorality.

*'"Come, I will show you the punishment of the great
prostitute, who sits on many waters. With her the kings of
the earth committed adultery and the inhabitants of the
earth were intoxicated with the wine of her adulteries" ...
She held a golden cup in her hand, filled with abominable
things and the filth of her adulteries.'*

(Revelation 17:1, 4)

The prostitute is an intelligent combination of all false religions and occult movements that seek world domination by
seducing leaders and by breaking down the morals of the
people of the earth. Those who have sold themselves to Satan
have already drawn up their plans, and have been carrying
them out for a very long time. In order to conquer the world, it
has been necessary for them to break down everything that
holds people together.

If family homes were securely held together in unity, if
young people had firm moral principles, if husbands were
faithful to their wives, the anti-Christian powers could never
take us over. It is the family and God's holy laws, the ten
commandments, that are a protection against revolutions,
wars, and dictators. But as soon as lawlessness is allowed its
way, people lose their vigilance, their fighting spirit.

The prophets of Baal acted according to this pattern. The

Asherah cult involved cult-prostitution and group sex, and through its seducing spirit the forces of darkness succeeded in gaining power over Israel in the time of Elijah.

The conspiracy of lawlessness in Elijah's time

Elijah's time is a prophetic type or pattern of the last days of the church in our own time. The seizure of Naboth's vineyard by Ahab and Jezebel is a prophetic action that helps us to understand the Antichrist conspiracy in the End Time.

When king Ahab was unable to get what he wanted from Naboth, Jezebel made her plan. She sent a letter to the elders and nobles of Naboth's town, written in Ahab's name and sealed with his seal. The loyalty of those leading men to the king and his family was a necessary requirement for the plot to succeed. The elders of the town were the religious leaders, and the nobles were the political, economic and administrative leadership. They found two rogues to give the necessary false evidence against Naboth, two members of the town Mafia. They proclaimed a fast, thereby giving the whole proceeding a cloak of religious respectability. They invited Naboth to the consequent gathering. After that, the secret conspiracy of lawlessness went ahead at full speed, breaking one after another of God's laws. The two rogues gave their false evidence, and said that Naboth had cursed both God and the king. *'You shall not give false testimony against your neighbour.'* Naboth was stoned to death although he was innocent. *'You shall not murder.'* Ahab took possession of Naboth's vineyard. *'You shall not covet your neighbour's house.'*

Where did these people get the courage that enabled them to break God's laws and standards in this way? If people have a sense of group unity and co-operation, they can derive strength and security from it. We can see too that the economic crime and murder were fruits of the conspiracy between the royal house, the religious leaders, the business people, and the Mafia.

The Antichrist conspiracy

Psalm 2 is a key scripture in describing the rebellion of the Antichrist. Those taking part in the conspiracy include the kings, the princes or men of power, and the judges. The rebellion is aimed at the casting aside of God's laws, which he has given to men. They are thrown off like fetters and bonds from which the captive longs to be free. The rebellion is also aimed at creating lawlessness. The Lord laughs at this rebellion, and prepares to crush it with his sceptre of iron, but before giving vent to his wrath he gives the rebel leaders a chance to repent and kiss the Son. He urges the kings to be wise, and the princes or judges to be warned.

Paul knew that lawlessness comes in as a secret power, as it was already doing in his time (2 Thessalonians 2:7). Psalm 2 shows that it comes in as a conspiracy, with the kings and princes taking counsel together against the Lord. We can conclude therefore that lawlessness comes over the earth as a secret conspiracy between kings, judges, and leaders.

The process that has led to the de-Christianising of our western European society, to the discarding of the ten commandments, to the denial of the sanctity of marriage, and to the breaking of the laws of creation by opening the way for homosexuality, is all the result of a political and religious conspiracy of the kind that we have had for hundreds of years through such secret orders as the Masons and the Knights Templars. Among their members have been kings, presidents and religious leaders from all religions, together with the Mafia.

The conspiracy against Jesus

Who were the people who conspired against Jesus? The apostles named them in their prayer (Acts 4:23–31) which actually quotes Psalm 2. They were the Jews and the Romans, the Sanhedrin with the elders and chief priests, Herod, and Pilate. The renegade Judas joined the conspiracy. Some evil men were given immunity from prosecution to persuade them to testify falsely against Jesus. Herod and Pilate became friends in a common purpose of putting Jesus to death. Pilate was being threatened. The people were stirred up by the leaders into shouting: 'Crucify! Crucify!' When we learn about Satan's planning, he no longer appears particularly inventive; in his later planning, he is inclined to revert to his earlier patterns.

The conspiracy in the last times

Revelation 17–18 tells of the last great Antichrist conspiracy. The various parties to this conspiracy are:

1. The kings of the earth, who are led astray through sexual immorality into becoming a part of the conspiracy (Revelation 17:2; 18:3).
2. The occult religions. The prostitute is the mother of all prostitutes. She is the false and dead church, the occult movement in Judaism, together with all other occult religions and delusions.
3. The merchants of the earth. *'Your merchants were the world's great men'* (Revelation 18:23; 18:3).
4. Those who practise witchcraft and sorcery (Revelation 18:23). *'By your magic spell all the nations were led astray.'*
5. The dragon: Satan and Antichrist.

This conspiracy is a mystery, a secret long kept hidden. On the forehead of the great prostitute, a title was written that bore a secret meaning: *'Mystery: Babylon the great'* (Revelation 17:5).

Chapter 6

Jezebel of Tyre –
Elijah's Most Formidable Enemy

Elijah's worst enemy was Jezebel. She invoked her own gods
as a witness and backing when she threatened Elijah's life
(1 Kings 19:1–2). Elijah and Elisha won the victory over her.
We have said earlier that the events surrounding Elijah's life
follow a prophetic pattern, which is going to be repeated on a
larger scale in the last times. If we examine Jezebel from this
standpoint, it will help us to understand the great enemy of the
kingdom of God and the church – Babylon, the great prostitute of Revelation 17–18, who is like Jezebel in so many
ways.

Jezebel came from the city of Tyre. She was born at a time
when the ruling house of Tyre was notorious for its cruelty and
at the same time for its fervent worship of Baal and Astarte.
Jezebel's father Ethbaal came to power by murdering the
reigning king. He was both king of Tyre and high priest of the
goddess Astarte, the latter post giving him a status something
like that of a manager of a sex club. Astarte was worshipped
through sex orgies and temple prostitution. When Ethbaal
gave his daughter in marriage to the king of Israel, it was his
objective to increase the influence of the demonic powers over
Israel through the false gods Baal and Astarte or Asherah.
Immediately after the marriage ceremony, Ahab started to
serve Baal and worship him. He set up an altar for Baal in the
temple of Baal that he built in Samaria, and also made an

Asherah pole. He *'sold himself to do evil in the sight of the Lord, urged on by Jezebel his wife'* (1 Kings 21:25). Jezebel was a heathen in her whole character, and was skilled in magic. This was the judgment of Jehu upon her, when he charged her son Joram with reponsibility for his permissiveness: 'How can there be peace, as long as all the idolatry and witchcraft of your mother Jezebel abound?' (2 Kings 9:22).

Jezebel persecuted and killed every true prophet. Obadiah was forced to hide a hundred prophets in caves, so that they might escape from her persecution (1 Kings 18:4).

The prostitute in Revelation is equally bloodthirsty against the prophets: *'I saw that the woman was drunk with the blood of the saints, the blood of those who bore testimony to Jesus'* (Revelation 17:6); and John says of Babylon: *'In her was found the blood of prophets and of the saints, and of all who have been killed on the earth'* (18:24).

Jezebel set the pattern which the great prostitute followed, equally skilled in sorcery and idolatrous in character, and stamped in the same manner with the image of the city of Tyre. But they are also alike in that they can both be roused to furious anger.

Businessmen in collusion with Lucifer overcome the world

There is something demonic in the way the merchants of Tyre conducted their business. Even though they had no great military strength behind them, they were clever enough to dominate the trade of the whole Mediterranean area. They took a hand in the game when new kings came to power in the lands that traded with them. The merchants of Tyre were great men in the world, which means that they also had great political power (Isaiah 23:8–9). They controlled the barter trade between the sea-going countries, and they had as their trading agents Arabian princes and merchants from Sheba, Greece, Tubal and Meshech (Ezekiel 27).

The traders of Tyre were the first people named in the Bible as having the ambition to create a world kingdom of the kind that John sees in Revelation 18. It is necessary to read Ezekiel 26–28 in order to have a proper understanding of Revelation

18. Ezekiel understood that demonic powers lay behind the great success of the traders of Tyre in the world markets.

Ezekiel revealed that Tyre was a city in which Satan had power and influence over the government. The spirit of trade is directly linked with the fall of Satan. Ezekiel is told to say to the king of Tyre:

> 'You were the model of perfection ... you were in Eden, the garden of God ... you were anointed as a guardian cherub, for so I ordained you. You were on the holy mount of God ... You were blameless in your ways from the day you were created till wickedness was found in you. Through your widespread trade you were filled with violence, and you sinned ... By your many sins and dishonest trade you have desecrated your sanctuaries'
>
> (Ezekiel 28:12–18).

One of Satan's names is Mammon. He wants to be worshipped in the market-place through people putting their trust in money, materialism, and their own riches. Mammon wants to control the financial centres of the world and to turn the centres of trade into temples of Mammon.

When businessmen open themselves to the occult in order to become more successful in their business, then we have to be on our guard against demonic control in trade. There are businessmen these days who read their horoscopes to get guidance, company directors who take part in TM meditation, and business leaders who study hypnosis and parapsychology with a view to getting more pulling power in their advertising and in the rush for business. There are rock groups who hold satanic masses with blood sacrifices, dedicating their master recording so that it will be a sales success.

We have reached the stage when businessmen of the world, and bank directors, are prepared to make a covenant with Satan in order to gain greater influence in the world market; but this is also the stage when the prophetic Church needs to come forward and break the demonic spell over deluded mankind. God's spirit cries out for the restoration of the Elijah ministry!

Entering into a trade covenant with Satan

Our business should never be allowed to dominate us to such an extent that it decides the question whether we live or die. Satan wants to have everyone under covenant with him in order to buy and sell; that has always been the temptation held out by the Antichrist, and is not something new reserved for the last times, though it is exactly at that point that the whole of the world's inhabitants will be put to the test.

1. Solomon made a covenant with the king of Tyre, and became a Satan-worshipper. A friendship grew up between Hiram, king of Tyre, and Solomon, and they made a treaty with one another. It was a typical trade treaty, aimed at an exchange of goods. Hiram said, *'I will do all you want in providing the cedar and pine logs ... and you are to grant my wish by providing food for my royal household'* (1 Kings 5:8–9). This covenant was a political and economic treaty to help with the building of the temple in Jerusalem. Solomon did not realise that behind the trading capacity of Tyre there stood Satan himself. King Hiram gave his daughter in marriage to Solomon, and she was one of those who led Solomon astray into the worship of false gods. He started to follow Ashtoreth (Astarte) the goddess of the Sidonians (1 Kings 11:5). The satanists regard Solomon as their founder and as the first Satan-worshipper.

When the Antichrist makes a binding covenant with many people, it is a trade covenant on the same lines as the treaty that Hiram made with Solomon, in which Satan was the unseen third party. The Masons and other secret orders build all their covenants on the accounts of the covenant that was made between Solomon and Hiram of Tyre. Their key-word is tolerance and their vision is to continue building the temple of Solomon into a place of worship for all religions. Their temple will be a platform for Antichrist to proclaim himself to be God.

2. The great test for the seven churches of Asia Minor, in Revelation 2–3, was how they would conduct themselves with the business community and the trade guilds that had false gods as their protectors. In order to be able to buy and sell,

they were compelled to take part in ceremonial meals in which meat was eaten that had been sacrificed to idols, and the meals ended with sex orgies. It is against this background that we need to read the letter to Thyatira (Revelation 2:18–29) which describes how the temptation of Jezebel comes to try to mislead the members of the church into sexual immorality and the eating of food sacrificed to idols. This teaching, which Jezebel represented, included 'Satan's so-called deep secrets', that is, black magic. Those Jews who had sold themselves to Satan were influential in this trade guild, and were therefore called 'the synagogue of Satan'. In Pergamum, some of the church held to the teaching of Balaam with its sorcery. Those Christians who had not compromised their faith, by becoming involved with these business communities and trade guilds, began to live in poverty. This was the reason why the church of Smyrna was persecuted, and the church of Philadelphia was poor.

There have at all times been secret orders and trade societies which have enticed leaders and businessmen into joining. It was necessary to be a member of these secret orders in order to be able to buy and sell and to climb up the ladder. Often these societies have been infiltrated by the occult. Even in modern times there are businessmen who through the Masons have entered into covenants in the names of Baal, Osiris and Jehovah.

There is a continuity between Tyre in the time of Elijah, and Babylon, the great prostitute in the end time. Satan has been responsible for this continuity. His spirit is the spirit of trade, and he has always tried to build up his power over the world by means of that buying and selling that takes place on his terms. In Elijah's time, a man's well-being and success in the community depended on his bowing the knee to Baal and giving Baal the kiss of greeting. Those seven thousand who had not done this were shut out of the community, but they were God's special possessions, his trump-cards.

Elijah and Elisha, instruments of the judgment on Jezebel

Elijah and Elisha were never beaten by Jezebel. When Elijah's life was threatened by her, he fled to Horeb. The revelation of God's glory gave him new courage, and he was ordered by God to go back to the scene of action, where Jezebel and all her intrigues were to be found.

In the presence of Ahab, Elijah pronounced the Lord's judgment on Jezebel, as they stood together on Naboth's piece of land. *'And also concerning Jezebel the Lord says: "Dogs will devour Jezebel by the wall of Jezreel"'* (1 Kings 21:23)

When Elijah was at Horeb, he was given the task of anointing two men to be kings. Hazael was to be anointed king of Aram, and Jehu the son of Nimshi was to be anointed king of Israel. These two men were to be God's instruments for the execution of his judgment on Jezebel and the house of Ahab. Elijah in turn left this task to be carried out by Elisha.

Later on, Elisha sent a young prophet to anoint Jehu and to convey to him the prophetic message that he was to be an instrument of the condemnation of the house of Ahab and of Jezebel. Through Jehu, the Lord would avenge the blood of all his servants the prophets (2 Kings 9:1–13).

Jehu became the means of carrying out the death sentence on Joram also, because Joram had been so lenient towards his mother Jezebel's heathen customs and her witchcraft. Jehu met Joram at the plot of ground that had belonged to Naboth, and after he had killed Joram, he reminded his chariot officer of how Elijah's word of judgment on the house of Ahab had been fulfilled on Naboth's actual plot of land. We must praise the Lord for his righteous judgments (2 Kings 9:14–26). Jehu was also the means of destroying all the remaining prophets of Baal (2 Kings 10:18–31). Through Jehu, Baal was exterminated from Israel, and the prophecy of Elijah against Jezebel was fulfilled (2 Kings 9:30–37).

If we translate this prophetic pattern into end-time terms, we see that it is through the Elijah ministry, through the prophetic Church, that the judgment will be pronounced against the world system of Antichrist. The Church is to anoint the instruments of judgment, and to pray people into action who will be those instruments and will execute judgment on the occult movements and the satanic world economic system. The Lord will avenge the blood of his servants the prophets.

The prophetic Church will see to it that the great prostitute and the great city of Babylon are actually destroyed. We shall not simply stand and blame God for allowing the satanic world system to continue for so long. The restoration of the Elijah ministry is needed so that, in co-operation with the Lord, the world can be made free and the way prepared for the coming of God's kingdom.

The Lord's strategy for victory over the great prostitute

In order to win the victory over the Antichrist system, God's Word gives us a strategy, and provides an instruction manual for the victorious Church in the last days.

1. People of God must be found who are willing to rely completely on the Lord for their provision. Elijah was willing to renounce normal society for three and a half years, trusting that God would provide for all his needs. First he was provided for at the Kerith ravine, then in the company of the widow of Zarephath. People must be found who are willing to live outside the economic system controlled by Antichrist. If there are no such people willing to live outside the system, then the system can never be destroyed. The world must see the difference between the economy of the Kingdom and Satan's economic system, and there must be a clear separation between these two systems so that God's kingdom can come (Malachi 3). The main battlefield in the end time will be the world economy, and there the prophetic Church must be involved, to demonstrate God's Kingdom-economy.

2. People of God must be found, who have heard in their spirits the cry of judgment over Babylon. The Lord is going to reveal his judgment against Babylon to his own people, long before it takes effect. Several times in Revelation there comes a cry of judgment from heaven against the prostitute. *'A second angel followed and said, "Fallen! Fallen is Babylon the Great, which made all the nations drink the maddening wine of her adulteries"'* (Revelation 14:8). When you hear the cry for the first time, the judgment is going to fall on your own life and your own economy; but on the second occasion, you will stand in freedom, outside the power of the satanic world

government, and will hear the cry of judgment against a society that will suddenly come to ruin when God's wrath strikes it. Like Elijah, we shall be ready to pronounce judgment against the prostitute and to pray into action the instruments of judgment.

3. The call must go out to everyone involved with Babylon to come out from it. The prophetic Church must pass on the call that comes from heaven. *'Then I heard another voice from heaven say: "Come out of her, my people, so that you will not share in her sins, so that you will not receive any of her plagues"'* (Revelation 18:4).

4. A final battle is coming, but the prophetic Church will not begin the battle. It will be begun by the prostitute, the beast, and the kings of the earth.

> *'They will make war against the Lamb, but the Lamb will overcome them because he is Lord of lords and King of kings – and with him will be his called, chosen and faithful followers.'* (Revelation 17:14)

Chapter 7

Compromise with a Defeated Enemy

A defeated enemy leads Ahab into compromise

Ahab won two victories over Ben-Hadad the king of Syria by following the guidance of the prophets, but in the end he fell into the enemy's trap and made a treaty with the defeated enemy (1 Kings 20).

The Bible says nothing by chance, even when names or figures are mentioned. The Jews believe that the events of Elijah's time form a prophetic pattern that will be repeated on a larger scale in the end time:

> 'These things happened to them as examples and were written down as warnings for us, on whom the fulfilment of the ages has come.'   (1 Corinthians 10:11)

God's Word is to be read prophetically, and interpreted according to the Spirit and not according to reason. The Bible is an instruction book for the last times, so that God's people will know how to meet everything as conquerors. The nearer we get to the close of the age, the more seals will be broken and secrets revealed. The more we get into trouble in the last times, the more we shall need prophetic guidance. There are many layers of revelation in God's word. The generations before us have received the revelation that they needed to be conquerors in their time. We need to have more revelation in order to be conquerors in the final stage.

There is prophetic guidance for us in this chapter, 1 Kings

20, which tells how the prophets guided Israel in battle, but also tells of the great mistake that Ahab made in making a compromise with a defeated enemy. Satan is a defeated enemy. It is when we have not fully grasped the greatness of Jesus' victory at Golgotha that we are outwitted by the enemy.

The king of Aram – a type of the Antichrist

When I speak of Antichrist, I do not just mean one single person. John said: *'As you have heard that the antichrist is coming, even now many antichrists have come'* (1 John 2:18). John calls this phenomenon *'the spirit of the antichrist, which you have heard is coming and even now is already in the world'* (1 John 4:3). Antichrist stands for a lawless type of man in the end time. When this lawless type of man has been formed, then there may also be, as the tip of the iceberg, an individual person. Antichrist stands as a definition of the enemy of the Church in the whole of the present age. The Church acts prophetically when it recognises and points out the real enemy.

Antichrist is the ruler of a kingdom that is at war with the kingdom of light. His kingdom is out to bring the whole world together under the power of Satan. Ben-Hadad, king of Aram (Syria) had assembled 32 kings to go to war with him against Israel. In this he is like Antichrist, who assembles kings and countries in battle against Israel. He is also like Antichrist in his totalitarian claims. His messengers came with this impudent, presumptuous assertion: *'This is what Ben-Hadad says: "Your silver and gold are mine, and the best of your wives and children are mine"'* (1 Kings 20:3). Antichrist will come with a total claim to take control over our economy and over our families. He will make this demand for control on the strength of his impudence. Ben-Hadad's messengers came again with an even more impudent demand: *'Deliver to me your silver and your gold, your wives and your children'* (20:5 RSV).

Ahab is a picture of the way in which many a head of government in the time of Antichrist will react, step by step, in the face of the enemy's demands for power. Ahab was submissive to Ben-Hadad. Ahab could be the prime minister of a country, reacting to the demands of Antichrist on the country's economy and its family relationships.

The prophets in leadership in the war against Ben-Hadad

When this totalitarian threat against Israel came, there was, thanks to Elijah's example and ministry, a new boldness in the prophets, who came forward to save the people. I would liken this to prayer warfare, which is also led by prophets who can hear the voice of the Lord. This is where I see scope for the prophetic Church. In a similar situation of war, king Jehoshaphat, after the song of praise had been used as a weapon, gave an example of prophetic leadership in prayer war when he stood and said: *'Have faith in the Lord your God and you will be upheld; have faith in his prophets and you will be successful'* (2 Chronicles 20:20).

A prophet came forward to Ahab and announced, *'This is what the Lord says: "Do you see this vast army? I will give it into your hand today, and then you will know that I am the Lord"'* (1 Kings 20:13). The same prophet directed Ahab as to how the battle should be fought and who should represent Israel in it. Ahab asked who should be chosen to lead the arm of Israel, and the prophet replied, *'The young officers of the provincial commanders will do it'*. So Ahab summoned 232 young officers and appointed them as leaders in the battle against Ben-Hadad, the Antichrist of that age.

The prophetic Church's war against the spirit of Antichrist and its anti-Christian leaders in our own countries will be led by the younger generation. The older generation are so bound up in these times by consumer spending, by buying and selling, that they will have a hard time getting free from the economic system of Antichrist. The younger people are not so concerned about whether they will buy and sell or not. The young people, too, are not so bound up with secret societies such as Freemasons, Knights Templars, and so on, which will hold many of the older people bound when the time arrives for Antichrist to come forward. He will be able to form a powerful brotherhood with those that are already bound by these loyalties. But the young people have no such loyalties, and they can be mobilised to form the new, young army of the Lamb.

> *'Your people will offer themselves freely on the day you
> lead your host upon the holy mountains. From the womb
> of the morning like dew your youth will come to you.'*
>
> (Psalm 110:3 RSV)

The Lord will assemble a young army of undestroyed character, when he is ready to put his enemies under his feet.

Ahab also summoned 7,000 of the men of Israel. We do not
know much about these men. Why did Ahab assemble so few
against such an enormous opposing force? It was a chosen
group, the same number of men, 7,000, as those Elijah was
told of on Mount Horeb, when he complained to God that he
was the only prophet left, saying, *'The Israelites have ... put
your prophets to death with the sword. I am the only one left,
and now they are trying to kill me too.'* At this point, Elijah
was corrected by the Lord. *'Yet I reserve seven thousand in
Israel – all whose knees have not bowed down to Baal and all
whose mouths have not kissed him'* (1 Kings 19:14, 18).

Paul comments on this passage: *'So too, at the present time
there is a remnant chosen by grace'* (Romans 11:3–5). The
Lord has a chosen army, whom he has shielded from compromise with the god of this age. Those who were hidden away by
the Lord, during the terrorism of Jezebel and the prophets of
Baal, would have included the hundred prophets who were
hidden fifty at a time in a cave.

The army that was assembled against Ben-Hadad consisted
of young leaders, a chosen force of men who had not compromised themselves, and a group of prophets who gave guidance. Through this army, a great victory was won over Ben-
Hadad and his 32 subordinate kings. A great defeat was
inflicted on both the horses and the chariots of the enemy.

Prophetic information was also given to Ahab after his
victory, when he was told that Ben-Hadad would return with a
fresh attack the following year.

The Arameans attack a second time

When Ben-Hadad the king of Aram prepared himself for his
next assault on Israel, he appeared to have a very strange

concept of God, which the Lord himself regarded as a great insult. He thought that God was a god of the hills and not of the plains. This was a distinctive sign of the Antichrist spirit, saying in effect that God is only one of many gods. The Freemasons place the Lord on an equal footing with Osiris and Baal; this spirit is that of Antichrist, and we recognise it also in Ben-Hadad's way of speaking about God. This concept of God as being only a god of the hills can be translated into present-day terms: 'You can stay happily in your churches with your faith in God on Sundays, but don't let your faith get mixed up with your daily life, your place of work, or your community.' I know of an example of this anti-Christian concept: a Swedish Christian doctor was stopped by his Social Board from praying with his patients, even those who asked for prayer, in the hospital surgery. It is acceptable for the Bible to be found in a Church, but it was not permitted in a certain children's day centre. God is thought of as a church-god but not as an everyday God.

This insult to God led to Ben-Hadad being defeated once again. God fought against Ben-Hadad, not in order to help Ahab but for the sake of his own honour. A man of God came up and told the king of Israel,

> *'This is what the Lord says: "Because the Arameans think the Lord is a god of the hills and not a god of the valleys, I will deliver this vast army into your hands, and you will know that I am the Lord."'* (1 Kings 20:28)

It is a characteristic of Antichrist that he sets himself up against all that is holy, and against all authority. When Ben-Hadad came against Israel the second time, he had removed all the 32 kings from their commands and replaced them with other officers. Translated into today's terms: Antichrist deceives and manipulates the world's leadership, and draws them into his circle of influence by means of tricks, promises of careers, power, sex, riches, or by threats or using the language of force. But very soon he removes all those in authority and replaces them with others who suit his system better. The world will come to be divided into ten regions and will be governed by a federation of ten kings. Many of those who are working today for a new economic world order are serving the purpose of a world government, but they will eventually be removed and liquidated when the power take-over by Antichrist has taken place.

The Arameans came and filled the land with their army. The people of Israel were also mustered, and camped opposite the enemy like two small herds of goats. There is going to be a day in the last times, when an army of the Lord consisting of believing Jews will be camped together with the prophetic Church against the kingdom of Antichrist. There will be one flock and one shepherd. This unity is already realised when we love Israel because of the promises given to their fathers. We love them because we know that they will one day turn to the Lord and become a kingdom of kings and priests.

Ben-Hadad began this battle by insulting God. Once again the Lord gave Israel a great victory over the Arameans, who sustained 100,000 casualties. The rest of them escaped to the town of Aphek, where the wall collapsed on 27,000 of them. The ten kings in Antichrist's federation will make war against the Lamb, but the Lamb will fight together with his called, chosen and faithful followers, and will overcome them (Revelation 17:14). He who abuses the Lord finds out that the battle is the Lord's.

Compromise and covenant with a defeated enemy

Ben-Hadad was now a defeated enemy. His army had been annihilated, and he himself fled into the town and hid in an inner room. His only way out was to use cunning. He could at least persuade Ahab to feel sorry for him. So his officials put on sackcloth around their waists and ropes around their heads, and pleaded with Ahab for Ben-Hadad's life. Now came Ahab's compromise: he called Ben-Hadad his brother. *'Is he still alive? He is my brother'*. It ended with Ahab renewing his brotherly treaty with Ben-Hadad, as a trading agreement. Ben-Hadad dictated the conditions even though he was the loser. *'I will return the cities my father took from your father.*

You may set up your own market areas in Damascus, as my father did in Samaria'. Ahab made a pact with Ben-Hadad and set him free. Ahab's mistake was that he did not seek counsel from the Lord after he had won the victory. Earlier, the prophets had saved him by their advice from defeat by a superior enemy (1 Kings 20:30–34).

We can read about one of the consequences of the treaty with Ben-Hadad in the story of Naboth's vineyard. Ahab made a claim against Naboth similar to that which Ben-Hadad had made against Ahab. Something of Ben-Hadad's spirit and mode of action was carried over into Ahab, and this became in the end the reason for Elijah pronouncing the final judgment on Ahab and his house. For those who make a treaty with Antichrist, there is no longer any hope of salvation.

Tough or cowardly prophets

Ahab had entered into a pact with a defeated enemy. Ben-Hadad had passed the limit where he had filled up the measure of his sins, and he was therefore under the judgment of God. He was condemned. God had decided on his annihilation. Ahab had made a compromise with someone who was under the wrath of God. How should a prophet bring this message home to Ahab?

We read in 1 Kings 20:35–43 of a tough young prophet whom the Lord had provided with an imaginative way of dramatising his message. The Old Testament prophets were dramatic in their way of presenting prophecies; Jeremiah went around carrying a heavy yoke; Ezekiel made a hole in the wall and brought out all his household goods as if he were a fugitive from a besieged city. The tough young prophet went to his companion and said, *'Strike me, I pray'* (1 Kings 20:35 RSV). But his companion refused to strike him. And why? He wanted to be a respectable prophet. There are certain limits on how a prophet ought to behave. He must have been full of criticism and contempt for the rash young prophet, or the Lord would not have given him such a hard punishment. The first prophet had received his dramatic presentation from the Lord. The judgment fell on the traditional, cowardly prophet, who wanted everything to proceed quietly and tidily. *'"Because you have not obeyed the Lord, as soon as you leave me a lion will kill you". And after the man went away, a lion found him and killed him.'*

We cannot defeat the spirit of Antichrist in a tidy, religious manner. Jesus himself is prophetically seen in this battle, so blood-spattered and stained that sometimes his own people have trouble in recognising him (Isaiah 63:1–6).

But our tough young prophet found, as it turned out, another prophet of the same calibre. He received his bruise, and then disguised himself with his head-bandage, and went to Ahab with his stern message. The Lord gave him the idea of telling a story, and through the question he asked of Ahab he managed to get Ahab to pass judgment on himself and his own conduct. Ahab recognised him as one of the prophets as soon as he took the bandage off. Boldly he prophesied: *'This is what the Lord says: "You have set free a man I had determined should die. Therefore it is your life for his life, your people for his people."'* Sullen and angry, Ahab returned to Samaria.

Prophets with boldness and initiative are required to defeat Antichrist. A single one of the Lamb's redeemed ones with ideas and drive is worth more than a million men in the battle against the world kingdom of Antichrist.

Antichrist makes his conquests through compromise

Not by the might of armies, but through compromises, Antichrist will succeed in becoming for a short time the ruler of the world. For the lawless one there is always a practical way, since he has no values to hold on to. Ben-Hadad reached his goal through making extreme claims, through two confrontations, and through tempting Ahab into a compromise, a peace treaty which was broken three years later.

The decline of Christian faith in Sweden has always happened through compromise. Family legislation aimed at making divorce easier and allowing unmarried couples to live together, laws that have opened the way for pornography, the depiction of violence, blasphemy and the acceptance of homosexuality, have all the time been driven through by people seeking to follow a golden middle way in the committee reports. Christians have followed along with the compromises. Further confrontations have invariably advanced the cause of those who are the driving powers behind the de-Christianising of our country.

The method of compromise is to manipulate people's minds by making extreme demands, and then to meet the opposition halfway.

In occult literature there are many examples of compromise thinking. In the kingdom of darkness, good and evil are of equal value and a balance is arrived at when evil and good find one another. 'True justice unites goodness and strength, it is neither violent nor weak. Blessed are you if you understand these words, words from the spirit, which unite the right with the left, the higher with the lower. Opposite rules opposite, the extremists find contact, and the different forms belong together and act in relation to one another.' These words are quoted from a piece of New Age writing inspired by Lucifer and glorifying him.

One man who worked for Antichrist's power take-over, the American General Albert Pike, a member of the Illuminati group in USA, wrote the following in a letter to the Italian revolutionary leader Mazzini. The letter is dated 15th August 1871. In it he outlined plans for three world wars. He stated that in the third of these wars, 'we shall unleash the Nihilists and Atheists, and we shall provoke a formidable social cataclysm which in all its horror will show clearly to the nations the effect of absolute atheism, origin of savagery and of the most bloody turmoil. Then everywhere, the citizens, obliged to defend themselves against the world minority of revolutionaries, will exterminate those destroyers of civilization, and the multitude, disillusioned with Christianity, whose deistic spirits will from that moment be without compass [direction], anxious for an ideal, but without knowing where to render its adoration, will receive the pure light through the universal manifestation of the pure doctrine of Lucifer, brought finally out in the public view, a manifestation which will result from the general reactionary movement which will follow the destruction of Christianity and atheism, both conquered and exterminated at the same time.'

Lucifer is neither Christian nor godless, he is between the two. But he must unleash the anarchists, revolutionaries and atheists in order to force the Christians to begin to move away from their positions and thereby to undermine their faith.

Those who are preparing for Antichrist's power take-over are at work, manipulating extremes into prominence and from those extremes creating compromises, which correspond with their original purpose. The new world citizen, who will adapt to the kingdom of Antichrist, is a person of compromise, of lawlessness.

But the army that defeats the kingdom of Antichrist, the overcomers of Revelation, are described throughout as *'those who obey God's commandments and hold to the testimony of Jesus'* (Revelation 12:17). *'They did not love their lives so much as to shrink from death'* (12:11). They hold fast what they have, and they are faithful to death.

Chapter 8

A Nation Given Over to Lying Propaganda

By learning from the historic events during the lifetime of Elijah, and observing how the true prophets acted, I am seeking strategies for prophetic action in the End Time. King Ahab, at the end of his life, was surrounded by prophets who spoke lies. The Lord had put a deceiving spirit into the mouths of all his prophets, so that they prophesied lies (1 Kings 22:22). Our spiritual battlefield in the End Time will be nations given over to lying propaganda through their media, their education, their experts and their leaders.

I have lived in a nation where the media have glorified the communist regimes and have believed in the lies of communism. Those who believed in another reality were called reactionary. When we reported about Jewish refuseniks and the persecuted underground Church, we were not always believed, and were accused of scaremongering about the Soviet Union.

The media pass on the PLO propaganda against Israel, and it is very seldom that people are allowed to hear the truth about Israel. As Bible-believing Christians we can identify with Israel, because the media are treating us in the same way – distorting the truth.

We are being prepared for a time when a world dictator will be given a mouth speaking arrogant words and blasphemies (Revelation 13:5). That mouth will give him an ability to deceive those who dwell on the earth with his propaganda machine.

The corporation of prophets

Before Ahab and Jehoshaphat, the kings of Israel and Judah, went out into battle against the king of Aram, they sought counsel from the Lord (1 Kings 22:5–8). So the king of Israel brought together the 400 prophets, and asked them to advise whether they should go to war against Ramoth Gilead. All the prophets answered, *'Go, for the Lord will give it into the king's hand'*. The two kings sat on their thrones dressed in their royal robes, and the prophets prophesied in front of them, all of them to the same effect, but neither Ahab nor Jehoshaphat was inclined to rely on them.

The messenger who went to summon the prophet Micaiah also carried a secret message to him from the company of prophets:

> *'Look, as one man the other prophets are predicting success for the king. Let your word agree with theirs, and speak favourably.'* (1 Kings 22:13)

The 400 were lying prophets. They did not have that freedom from fear of men that is the characteristic mark of the army of the Lamb. They were concerned to ensure that all the prophets spoke with a uniform voice, and wanted Micaiah to conform. They were Ahab's men; they had become court prophets. The mark of a false prophet is that he prophesies good fortune for those whom God has judged unfavourably. Both Elijah and another prophet had pronounced judgment on Ahab and his house.

The prophetic Church must stand economically free from the authorities of the nation, or it will acquire wrong loyalties. In my nation, most churches receive support from the state. All who belong to the Lutheran church pay a church tax as part of their income tax. The state, in the name of equality, also pays non-Lutheran churches a certain fee for every member. There are a few churches who refuse to receive Government aid because they want to be a free prophetic voice in the nation.

Taken over by a lying spirit

The prophet Micaiah had seen in a vision an explanation of why all the other prophets had spoken the same message. The Lord had given permission for a lying spirit to lure Ahab into disaster, and to become a lying spirit in the mouth of all of Ahab's prophets (1 Kings 22:19–23).

When God condemns people to be taken over by a lie, it is not something that happens without reason. This judgment came on people who had not made room for the truth. The reason why people will be deceived by Antichrist, who comes with all the signs and wonders appropriate to his lie, is:

> *'They refused to love the truth and so be saved. For this reason God sends them a powerful delusion so that they will believe the lie and so that all will be condemned who have not believed the truth but have delighted in wicked-ness.'*   (2 Thessalonians 2:10–12)

Several prophets had come with messages of truth to Ahab, before he was taken over by the lie.

The apostle John saw the struggle between the kingdoms of light and of darkness as a battle between the truth and a lie:

> *'But you have an anointing from the Holy One, and all of you know the truth ... Who is the liar? It is the man who denies that Jesus is the Christ. Such a man is the antichrist – he denies the Father and the Son.'*   (1 John 2:20, 22)

John sees marks of likeness between liar and Antichrist.

The event described in Revelation that most closely corres-ponds with Ahab's enticement by lying spirits into going to war, is in Revelation 16:13–14:

> *'Then I saw three evil spirits that looked like frogs; they came out of the mouth of the dragon, out of the mouth of the beast and out of the mouth of the false prophet. They are spirits of demons performing miraculous signs, and they go out to the kings of the whole world, to gather them for the battle on the great day of God Almighty.'*

The Lord had everything under control when he determined the day for execution of his judgment on Ahab. In the same way, the Lord has everything under control when he determines his day of judgment on Antichrist and the leaders and nations that have followed him. They will be called together by lying spirits.

Jesus warned of those who will be the instruments of the lie in the last days:

> *'For false Christs and false prophets will arise and show great signs and wonders, so as to lead astray, if possible, even the elect.'* (Matthew 24:24 RSV)

Hypocritical liars with seared consciences

> *'The Spirit clearly says that in later times some will abandon the faith and follow deceiving spirits and things taught by demons. Such teachings come through hypocritical liars, whose consciences have been seared as with a hot iron. They forbid people to marry ...'*
> (1 Timothy 4:1–3)

What did Paul know of a society that would abolish marriage? 400 years before Christ, a dialogue took place between Socrates and Plato about a state in which marriage would be abolished. The women would be the property of everyone, and children would be brought up by the state in a way rather like today's nursery school or children's day centre. The children would anyway be the property of the state, and would not know who their real parents were, nor would the parents know who their children were. Plato further described a society with free sex, naked women, abortion of unwanted children, euthanasia and a legal right to get rid of the handicapped.

Plato described how the ruling class in society would manipulate people into believing in myths. They would talk of brotherhood, but in practice people would be forced to accept class divisions. Mankind would be divided into gold, silver, copper and iron. The lower classes would, however, not want to have so many children, so that the development of society would be directed towards the lower classes having fewer children.

The kind of society that Plato dreamed of is being brought into being in nations, through lying propaganda with even some Christians taking part in it. The undermining of the family has succeeded so far that we have school classes today where more than half of the children come from divorced families. There are politicians, businessmen and scientists today who are working hard to bring into being the kind of society that Paul warns us about.

According to Paul, we shall have a difficult time in exposing these lies of Antichrist, particularly those arising from within our own ranks. The Bible warns of false prophets, false teachers, people taking refuge in lies, false saviours. We must realise that the lie is generated in a mixture of politics and the occult, the kind of mixture of which Freemasonry is a typical example, with so many of the leaders of our western countries involved in it.

Through the exposing of the Italian Masonic Lodge P2 in 1981, which brought down the government of the time in Italy, and through documents that came to light in connection with it, we were able to get some idea of the extent of infiltration of the Roman Catholic church by Freemasons. Francesco Marchisano, the under-secretary of the congregation for Catholic education and a Mason since 1961, sent a letter in 1966 to the Italian Grand Master. He stated in it that 'yesterday evening' – the letter was dated in October – there had been a meeting at which it had been decided to start an experiment in the Italian seminaries for the training of priests. The intention was to spread the view that mankind is free and of value without any need for sovereignty or law. He emphasised the need for press support, and he urged that a meeting should be called to decide who should be entrusted with the various tasks. After this letter, it is possible to see how conditions changed in the seminaries. They were secularised. The Freemasons' and Marxists' plans were clear. They wanted to destroy the Church's faith by attacking the Church's heart, the training of priests.

These things give us an insight into the way that de-Christianising occurs in other countries too, through secret societies, by the arranging of a press campaign to prepare the way for, say, homosexual marriage, or the breaking-up of the custom of having a family surname, and so on.

The society of Antichrist is a society of a lie

The lie is spread around through the mass media, through education in schools, through culture, and through Christians who take part in these things.

> *'Why is my language not clear to you? Because you are unable to hear what I say. You belong to your father, the devil, and you want to carry out your father's desire. He was a murderer from the beginning, not holding to the truth, for there is no truth in him. When he lies, he speaks his native language, for he is a liar and the father of lies.'*
>
> (John 8:43–44)

The lie comes from speaking one's own words. God's word is truth. God's word endures until heaven and earth pass away. God's word must stand over the news agency, the message of the mass media, and the political propaganda. *'If anyone speaks, he should do it as one speaking the very words of God'* (1 Peter 4:11). The one sent from God speaks God's word.

Continue in the teaching of Christ, urges the apostle John:

> *'Many deceivers, who do not acknowledge Jesus Christ as coming in the flesh, have gone out into the world. Any such person is the deceiver and the antichrist. Watch out that you do not lose what you have worked for, but that you may be rewarded fully. Anyone who runs ahead and does not continue in the teaching of Christ does not have God; whoever continues in the teaching has both the Father and the Son.'*
>
> (2 John 7–9)

Micaiah – the free voice of truth

Micaiah stands as an example of the fact that it is still possible to be a prophetic voice even when a whole nation's leadership is given over to a lying spirit. It is true that Micaiah had first to be freed from the power of the lie. Through a vision of what was happening in the council of the angels, the Lord allowed him to get a true picture of what was happening in Israel (1 Kings 22:19).

Micaiah was free. He was willing to stand alone, to be a prophet of truth. He was slapped in the face by the leader of the company of prophets, who relied on his monopoly of ownership of the Spirit within his company. *'Which way did the spirit from the Lord go when he went from me to speak to you?'* he asked. Micaiah replied, *'You will find out on the day you go to hide in an inner room'* (22:24–25).

Micaiah has a near-namesake, the prophet Micah, who lived much later but speaks as if he was living in the same situation:

> *'This is what the Lord says: As for the prophets who lead my people astray, if one feeds them, they proclaim "peace"; if he does not, they prepare to wage war against him. Therefore night will come over you, without visions, and darkness, without divination. The sun will set for the prophets, and the day will go dark for them. The seers will be ashamed and the diviners disgraced. They will all cover their faces because there is no answer from God. But as for me, I am filled with power, with the Spirit of the Lord, and with justice and might, to declare to Jacob his transgression, to Israel his sin.'*
>
> (Micah 3:5–8)

The prophetic Church, in the midst of the battle against the community of Antichrist, will also be able to wage war on the false prophets. Before God's kingdom breaks in, several of the prophets speak of this sort of confrontation: see Jeremiah 23:9–22, Ezekiel 13 and Zechariah 13:2–3. Among the false prophets I include those who explain away the prophetic word. They say, 'The book of Revelation was written to Christians in the first century and has no relevant message for Christians today. It cannot be used as a blueprint for world history. The promises and the prophetic word in the Old Testament cannot be applied to the Middle East situation today.' They mislead Christians who need a clear understanding of the prophetic word, to be able to take their bearings and find their way in a time of great shakings and changes.

The prophetic Church must be able to point out the true enemy, and to show on what level the battle must be fought. From now until the final crisis, we shall stand against the lying spirit, so as to free people from the kingdom of darkness and bring them in under the truth in Jesus Christ, who will make them free.

If we do not fight against Antichrist's kingdom of lies, then we cannot save many people in the great harvest opportunity in the last times. If we can, in a right way, fight against the lying spirit over our country, then hundreds of thousands of our countrymen will be saved and will come flooding into the kingdom of God.

Chapter 9

Elijah – the Instrument of Israel's Restoration

On Mount Carmel, Elijah was the instrument in leading Israel to repentance. When the time comes for the return of the Messiah to the earth, Elijah will once again be the instrument of their turning their hearts back to the Lord.

The disciples asked Jesus after his resurrection: *'Lord, are you at this time going to restore the kingdom to Israel?'* (Acts 1:6). They did not then know the times and the hours that the Father had determined. The person with Elijah's calling always has the question in his heart: Am I living in the time when the kingdom will be restored to Israel? How near are we to the time when the people of Israel will recognise their Messiah? How is the restoration of Israel going to happen?

Many Christians have a theology in which this is a problem that does not concern them, since it is something that they leave behind them at Jesus' coming, something that concerns Jesus himself, but the Church does not need to bother about it. Paul teaches in Romans 9–11 that the Church is involved in the conversion of Israel. According to God's plan, Israel will be awakened into envy through what they see of God's love poured out over the Church. Through the full number of the Gentiles coming in, all Israel will be saved. This 'pleroma', the fullness of the Gentiles, is not merely a total figure, but also a quality. When the Church reaches full maturity, the fullness of Christ, that maturity will be the releasing factor that will enable Israel to recognise their Messiah and be converted.

We need to realise that what happens to you and me in the way of spiritual growth and maturity contributes to the conversion of Israel. If we take seriously our prayer that God's kingdom should come on earth, then the conversion of Israel becomes an absolute priority for us, a heart desire, until we see our hope fulfilled. There can be no kingdom of peace on earth without a restored Israel.

Jewish expectations about the coming of Elijah

We shall examine some of the expectations that the Jews hold in connection with Elijah's coming. These arise partly from the rabbis' interpretations surrounding the scriptural account of Elijah, but also partly from legends and fanciful speculations. They are in any case evidence of the strong expectation of the Messiah that has been held by the Jews for thousands of years; while the Old Testament closes with the promise that Elijah will be sent before the great and dreadful day of the Lord.

Elijah is presented in Jewish expectations as the one who is forever watching over Israel's interests. He ministers as a mediator between God and the people. He is the link that connects the present time, with all its crises, needs, difficulties and possibilities, with the time of the Messiah to come.

Elijah is the forerunner of the coming Messiah. Jewish traditions say that Moses and Elijah will return in the same single person in the day of the Messiah. The Jews saw profound parallels between Moses and Elijah. Both took part in the freeing of Israel. Moses was sent to Pharaoh and Elijah was sent to Ahab; both used works of power to free the nation, and both of them met with the Lord on Mount Sinai (Horeb).

Elijah will reveal himself at the time of the battle with Gog and Magog. He will comfort Israel in her pain after all the sufferings she has gone through. He is likened to an angel sent out to drive away the superior enemy forces. When he comes, Israel will truly repent.

Elijah is tied to the consecration ceremony in the new covenant. He will give back to Israel everything that she has lost. In particular, there are three things that he will give back: the pot of manna, the vessel containing the oil of anointing and the secrets of its composition; and the vessel with the water of purification.

Elijah is to come three days before the coming of the Messiah. On the first day, he will stand on the mountains of Israel and proclaim: 'Peace comes to the world! Peace comes to the world!' On the second day he will call out: 'Goodness comes to the world! Goodness comes to the world!' Then on the third and last day he will shout: 'Salvation (Yeshua) comes to the world! Salvation comes to the world!' Then he will turn to Israel and say: 'See, your king comes to you!' Then Elijah will anoint the Messiah with the holy oil of anointing.

How far did the Jews' expectations of Elijah accord with John the Baptist?

John proclaimed that the kingdom of heaven was near, and led many people in Israel to repentance. He was the prophet of repentance on the bank of the Jordan.

He did indeed anoint the Messiah with the oil of anointing, but not at all in the way the rabbis had expected. He consecrated Jesus for his ministry by baptising him, and so Jesus was anointed, by the Holy Spirit coming down upon him.

In what way did John give back to Israel the things she had lost? Through baptism he gave her back the water of purification. He returned the vessel of anointing oil to her by pointing out Jesus as the one who would baptise with the Holy Spirit and with fire.

What about the manna? This was returned to Israel through the example of John in his manner of living. The reality of the manna was that God provided for his people in the desert. The spiritual secret of the manna was to dare to believe that God can be a father and a provider. John found everything that he needed in the way of clothing and food in the desert. He made clothes of camel-hair and he ate locusts and wild honey.

As the protector of Israel, Elijah confronted the prophets of Baal. John the Baptist confronted the Pharisees, and called them a generation of vipers.

John was a forerunner of the Messiah and prepared the way for Jesus in the hearts of the people. He called himself the friend of the bridegroom, whose task was to bring the bride and the bridegroom together.

The Signs of Elijah's Ministry to Israel

We shall go through the various signs of the Elijah ministry, as seen in the Jews' expectations, and ask ourselves how you and I, as members of the prophetic Church, can fulfil an Elijah ministry to Israel today.

Elijah is a watchman over the interests of Israel

After the Carmel experience, we see Elijah as an intercessor and a watchman. He prayed for rain, and for the blessing to return to Israel. Elijah climbed to the top of Carmel, bent down to the ground and put his face between his knees. Seven times he sent his servant to see if there was any sign of rain. At last the servant saw a cloud, as small as a man's hand. Then Elijah ran with joy ahead of Ahab's chariot, all the way to Jezreel (1 Kings 18:41–46).

This calling is ours also.

> *'I have posted watchmen on your walls, O Jerusalem; they will never be silent day or night. You who call on the Lord, give yourselves no rest, and give him no rest till he establishes Jerusalem and makes her the praise of the earth.'*
>
> (Isaiah 62:6–7)

To be a watchman today is to watch prophetically, that is, to compare the prophetic word with what is actually going on in Israel today. It is to follow all the news media you can find so as to know about the Jewish people. I know some who have gone into this watchman-ministry, who subscribe to the *Jerusalem Post* or some such newspaper that gives news of Israel. But the task of being a watchman is first and foremost a ministry of intercession for Israel, like that which Paul followed (Romans 10:1, 9:1–4).

Standing as a defender of Israel

To be a defender of Israel can seem like an impossible task. Yet it is one of the most important duties of one of the archangels: *'At that time Michael, the great prince who protects your people, will arise. There will be a time of distress ...'* (Daniel 12:1).

The angel Michael defends Israel. He has received his orders from God, and stands in direct confrontation with the powers of darkness in the heavenly places, in order to defend Israel in her last great time of need. This need arises because, among other things, all the nations of the earth will one day turn against Israel. Then there will be a need for people of God with the same calling as Michael. We shall defend Israel in her time of great need, and it is then that the ministry of Elijah will contribute to the conversion and salvation of her people.

It is no easy task to support Israel. They are both God's beloved people and also his enemies. If we look at them from the point of view of their attitude to the gospel, they are the enemies of God; but if we look at them according to the promises God has given to them, they are loved on account of the fathers (Romans 11:28). To defend them means standing against the powers and ideologies that seek to wipe them out. Israel has a calling of spiritual leadership among the nations, and the Lord has given them special gifts to enable them to fulfil that task. The gifts and the calling given to the Jewish people are irrevocable (Romans 11:29). Sometimes they have used their gifts for their own selfish purposes. There are times when the devil has used their gifts of leadership to the world. We defend them, however, because we know that when they come to God and get right with him, they will reach fulfilment in their calling to the world and become a great blessing to the nations.

Elijah – steward of the Messianic time to come

According to Jewish tradition, Elijah is the one who administers the Messianic future time. We are to be the bearers of the visions of God's Messianic kingdom, which are to be found in the prophetic books of the Old Testament. Many Jews have stopped believing; their hopes have been dashed too many times, and they have seen so many mistakes made among their own people. They have gone through so many crises of identity. We are to live in what they are one day going to be. Our love for them is based on that hope, founded on the Messianic promises.

Elijah will comfort Israel

Introducing the Elijah prophecy in Isaiah 40, the Lord says:

> *'Comfort, comfort my people, says your God. Speak tenderly to Jerusalem, and proclaim to her that her hard service has been completed, that her sin has been paid for, that she has received from the Lord's hand double for all her sins.'*

Our calling at the present time is to comfort the Jews; this is more important than to evangelise. They have so many wounds that have not been healed. They cannot forget the six million Jews who were destroyed by Hitler. Their unhealed wounds are one of the reasons why they cannot recognise the Messiah in Isaiah 53. The suffering servant is the Jewish people, they say. Their concentration on their own sufferings prevents them from seeing Jesus suffering on the cross.

> *'This is what the Lord says: "Your wound is incurable, your injury beyond healing. There is no one to plead your cause, no remedy for your sore, no healing for you ... But I will restore you to health and heal your wounds", declares the Lord, "because you are called an outcast, Zion for whom no one cares."'*
>
> (Jeremiah 30:12–13, 17)

God will use his people, who have the mind of Christ, to bring to fulfilment the promises he has made through the prophets. The Lord has promised Israel that she will be comforted, and he will give her that comfort through us.

'For this is what the Lord says: "I will extend peace to her like a river, and the wealth of nations like a flooding stream; you will nurse and be carried on her arm and dandled on her knees. As a mother comforts her child, so will I comfort you; and you will be comforted over Jerusalem."'   (Isaiah 66:12)

The Lord calls us to begin the fulfilment of this promise. You do not need to wait for the total restoration of the Jews in order to enter into your calling to be a comforter.

We shall comfort them by speaking to them prophetically of this hope, that their hard service has been completed, and that they will receive a double portion back from the Lord. Some have been given the gift of comforting Israel through prophetic songs, which they write and sing. To comfort Israel is to show them love in every conceivable way.

When will Elijah come?

In the Jewish tradition about the coming of Elijah, there are various different schools of thought. He will reveal himself on the same day that Messiah comes, says one rabbi, while another says he will come three days before. He will not come on a Sabbath eve, so as not to break the time of rest.

John the Baptist came forward six months before Jesus began his open ministry.

Elijah is coming when the Church reaches full maturity, attaining to the whole measure of the fullness of Christ (Ephesians 4:13). This fullness of Christ in the Church will be the condition for the release and conversion of Israel. Elijah will come when the prophetic Church has taken shape.

Elijah is the benefactor of Israel

In the Jewish tradition, the Elijah figure is a benefactor who follows Israel. Let us be benefactors of Israel! There is room for Gentile Christians to serve Israel according to the prophetic word. *'Foreigners will rebuild your walls, and their kings will serve you'* (Isaiah 60:10). Cyrus was a Gentile king who financed the building-up of Jerusalem after the Babylonian captivity. Many of us can serve together as Cyrus did and build up Jerusalem to become a spiritual, cultural and financial centre of the world. Visit Israel and its people; show them your love. Help the Jews from the former Soviet Union to return to their true homeland. Bring them on ships, planes and buses. Encourage the Jewish people from all nations to return to Israel. Invest your savings in State of Israel bonds. Never accept the Arab boycott. Buy and sell Israeli products. Even if the whole world agrees to impose sanctions on Israel, show Israel that there is one nation standing with them. Be ready to risk your life to protect a Jew in time of danger. In every need they have, when they need to be defended, when they need to know that they are not left alone, be creative and show that you are one who seeks the welfare of the Jews.

Elijah will give back to Israel what she has lost

In the Jewish tradition there is the expectation that Elijah will come with the pot of manna, the vessel containing the anointing oil, and the vessel with the water of purification, that is, the vessels that had disappeared from the temple. The vessels of the temple were prophetic pictures of spiritual realities. It is these realities, these forgotten manifestations of God's glory; the spiritual gifts of grace that were once in operation in Israel, the gifts of prophetic ministry and of miraculous powers, that the Elijah ministry will give back. All these things are being restored to the Church, which will awaken Israel to envy. They will realise what they have lost, and will accept these gifts back as their own.

Elijah is an ambassador to whom the Lord has given three keys

These keys are the miracle of feeding, the miracle of rainfall, and the power to awaken the dead to life. In the Jewish tradition, it is expected that Elijah will come forward as the Lord's ambassador, equipped with all the Lord's authority.

Elijah is like an angel who drives away the superior enemy forces

The rabbis expect Elijah to be like the angel who was sent out to drive away the superior army of the Assyrians, who besieged Jerusalem in the time of Hezekiah and Isaiah. The angel of the Lord at that time put to death 185,000 men in the Assyrian camp (Isaiah 37:36).

When Israel stands under the threat of her death as a nation, when all the nations of the world with their armies led by Gog and Magog swarm over the mountains of Israel, then the prayers of authority are needed, from people of prayer with the authority of Elijah, who can drive away the foreign armies. Through faith, foreign armies were routed (Hebrews 11:34). Elijah was in himself like a whole army of defence for Israel: *'My father! The chariots and horsemen of Israel!'* (2 Kings 2:12). This function of being an army of defence for Israel belongs also to the Elijah ministry.

Elijah will decide who is a Jew

According to Jewish tradition, Elijah will restore to their citizenship in Israel those who have been unrighteously, or by force, excluded from the community, but he will also exclude from Israel those who have falsely, or by force, come to belong to it.

Elijah excluded the prophets of Baal, and pronounced judgment on those who practised magic in accordance with Deuteronomy 18:9–13. There are those who belong to the synagogue of Satan, who claim to be Jews though they are not, but are liars (Revelation 3:9). Elijah has a ministry of distinguishing. When he comes, the distinction between the righteous and the wicked will be revealed. The arrogant and the evildoers will be burned in the furnace like stubble, but those who fear the Lord will be set free (Malachi 3:18; 4:1–2).

The Elijah ministry will bring together a restored Church and a converted Israel, and from these two there will be formed a single people.

> *'I have other sheep that are not of this sheep pen. I must*
> *bring them also. They too will listen to my voice, and there*
> *shall be one flock and one shepherd.'* (John 10:16)

The acceptance of the Jews will be life from the dead, and riches for the world (Romans 11:12–15). The light that the converted Jews will bring into the Church will cause a spiritual renewal and an enrichment for all living Christians.

Elijah will anoint Messiah with the holy anointing oil

John the Baptist consecrated Jesus for his public ministry through his baptism. The prophetic Church will in the same way anoint the Messiah through the Elijah ministry, through the Church's song of praise and worship. While the anti-Christian movement is under way and the rulers gather together against the Lord and his anointed one, there comes a warning to the world to honour the Son, lest he be angry. In fact we are warned to *'kiss the Son'* (Psalm 2). It is our worship of Jesus that anoints him as king over the earth. Make Jesus king in your prayers! Say to him, 'I know no other anointing than that with which the Holy Spirit has anointed you. You are anointed as king over all the earth; you are anointed as king over my country.'

The Elijah ministry goes into battle and exposes Israel's false leaders

Elijah exposed the false shepherds of Israel and attacked the prophets of Baal. Now, at the time of Messiah's coming, Israel has been led astray by false leaders. They have led Israel into a treaty with Antichrist, making a covenant with death and with the kingdom of death (Daniel 9:27; Isaiah 28:14–16). We should not be too surprised if there are Satan-worshippers among Jewish leaders, who have bowed the knee before him in order to obtain dominion over the world. To enable Satan to conquer the world, he needs the help of apostate Jews. There will be Jews in top positions in the government of Antichrist. We shall need to have demonstrated that we love the Jews with a faithful, steadfast love, before we can expose the false elders of Zion. The coming of Messiah will be a day of reckoning for those shepherds who only take care of themselves (Ezekiel 34).

Elijah will be the instrument of Israel's conversion

There is going to be a replay of the events on Mount Carmel. Through the Elijah ministry, Israel will have a choice set before her. Is it Jesus of Nazareth who is the Messiah, and are you going to receive him, or not?

I do not want to claim to be a prophet in the following description. I am only trying to represent a situation as it can be imagined, so that we shall understand how we can be involved in the salvation of Israel.

The time of decision comes when Israel is under threat of death, when annihilation is near. Israel is then surrounded by enemy armies, and there is no human help available. The Israeli leaders have a Samson complex, someone has said. Samson wanted to die with the Philistines. He bent the pillars of the house filled with Philistines, so that the house fell down and he killed many more when he died than while he lived (Judges 16:25–30). When all hope is gone, such present-day leaders are ready to wipe themselves out with an atomic weapon, but at the same time they are ready to draw the rest of the world into destruction with them. They are prepared to use nuclear weapons and at the same time to commit national suicide. They have no protection, because they have gone into the land without the protection of the blood. They have built up their state in their own strength, and therefore the state will become their cross.

When this threat of annihilation comes against Israel, Christians offer themselves as human shields to protect Jewish lives in Israel and all over the world, and very many Christians become martyrs. So many Christians die to protect Jews that their numbers surpass the 6 million Jews who died during Holocaust. This creates a new situation, where the Jews are ready to listen to the only kind of people who are willing to stand together with them, when the whole world is against them. Right in the middle of this death-agony, a delegation comes to seek audience with the military and political leaders of Israel. It is a group of Christians, representing the restored and prophetic Church throughout the world, the Church that lives and prays for Israel and whose members are willing to protect the Jews and risk their own lives. This group comes to fulfil the Elijah ministry, and the Lord will anoint some of the leaders of the group with a special authority. Israel is going to be faced with a choice. After some hours' time for consideration, the Israeli leaders are ready to accept Jesus as their Messiah, and they receive for themselves his sacrificial death as the Passover lamb, chosen by God for the turning away of the judgment of wrath from Israel. In the same moment as they receive Messiah, the whole military and political situation is turned around. The enemy armies are driven away.

Elijah's task of lifting off the covering and praying away the hardness of heart

Israel has experienced a hardening in part (Romans 11:25). Paul experienced this hardening:

> *'The Holy Spirit spoke the truth to your forefathers when he said through Isaiah the prophet: Go to this people and say, "You will be ever hearing but never understanding; you will be ever seeing but never perceiving." For this people's heart has become calloused; they hardly hear with their ears, and they have closed their eyes. Otherwise they might see with their eyes, hear with their ears, understand with their hearts and turn, and I would heal them.'*
>
> (Acts 28:25–27)

> *'Even to this day when Moses is read, a veil covers their hearts.'*   (2 Corinthians 3:15)

Anyone who accepts the Elijah responsibility needs to be continuously in intercession and prayer war against this dark cloud of obduracy to seek to disperse it, so that the sun of righteousness can arise over Israel. When God's time comes to remove the veil, the Lord will reveal the structure of the veil and give us understanding of the prayer strategy to use to co-operate with the Lord in removing it.

Chapter 10

Elijah's Ministry of Separation

The people in Elijah's time lived on the boundary between two kingdoms, the kingdom of God and the kingdom of Baal. They lived in this area because of their continual compromising. There were only 7,000 people in the whole land who had not compromised, who had not bowed the knee to Baal nor given him the kiss of greeting. The rest had done so, even though they were still believing that they were God's own people.

Into this religious shadow-land, created from concessions to Baal, Elijah entered, with a calling from God to separate. This separation began when Elijah confronted Ahab, who stands as a symbol of Antichrist. The separation begins now when some firm, bold person comes forward and says 'No' to Antichrist's system. This act creates a crisis which leads to a separation between God's kingdom and the kingdom of darkness.

How long will you waver between two opinions?

Elijah is himself involved in the making of a crisis that leads to a separation (1 Kings 18:19–24). Elijah wanted the people to choose which side they were on, but the people had nothing to say to him. They did not know the difference between the two kingdoms; they had not seen them separated, but only mixed together, and hence they were not yet ready to choose sides. Then came Elijah with his proposal to build two altars. The first was to be built by the prophets of Baal, and the other would be set up by Elijah himself. Then they would see on

117

which altar the fire of God would fall, and on which altar nothing would happen. The people agreed to this proposal.

When the prophets of Baal went around their altar from morning to evening, every person in Israel knew that this was a part of his life, in which he had lived and moved. People could identify with Baal-worship, but now they were seeing it in a new light, with its power and its magic removed. Now it appeared as empty religious machinery. In spite of many hours of limping around the altar, prophetic rage and much lacerating and tormenting of themselves, nothing happened. This altar, for us, represents dead works, self-chosen service for God. Heaven remains silent in the face of such efforts.

Elijah was at rest all through the day. He knew that the Lord was in control, and what he would do next; meanwhile he could mock the prophets from time to time. Then he prayed a prayer that the fire would fall, and the fire came down. Now came the separation; the glory of the Lord brought it into effect. Now it was easy for the people to choose. *'The Lord – he is God!'* they confessed. The evil was now easily disposed of. The prophets of Baal were tied up together like bundles of weeds ready to be carried away.

This separation needs to take place in our lives and in our churches. There needs to be a clear separation between that which God blesses and that which leaves him silent. We must pray this separation into being; indeed it has already begun. Dead religious activity has become like discarded machinery, and it has become much more noticeable that it does not have the glory of God upon it. It is as dead as the ritual procession of the prophets of Baal round their altar. At the same time, we are beginning to see on which altar it is that God's glory does fall, and we then have only to choose.

The time for separation

Despite all the good thoughts we entertain about the Church, there comes the morning of awakening when we see that amongst the good seed that has been sown, weeds are growing up. An enemy has come in and sown these weeds, and that enemy is the devil (Matthew 13:24–30, 37–43).

I have been involved in the building of churches both in Sweden and in Pakistan. It is always a group of enthusiastic people with a pioneering spirit who build a new church. They have God's vision for the new church that is to be born. It seems that the seed that has been sown is all good seed. But one day we wake up and find that there are weeds growing amongst the good seed. Should we then go and clear the weeds away? Jesus' answer to this question is:

> *'No, because while you are pulling the weeds, you may root up the wheat with them. Let both grow together until the harvest. At that time I will tell the harvesters: First collect the weeds and tie them in bundles to be burned; then gather the wheat and bring it into my barn.'*

In the same way, we should await the time for harvest, when the Lord gives the order to the harvesters.

My angel will prepare the way for me

Jesus says that the harvesters are angels, who will tie up the weeds into bundles and carry them away. It is like the punishment that was suffered by the prophets of Baal. In Jesus' parable it is the evildoers, those who have led people into lawlessness, that are represented by the weeds.

The ministry of Elijah, carried out through John the Baptist, is called *'my messenger* (angel) ... *who will prepare your way'* (Mark 1:2). In Malachi, chapters 3 and 4 describe Elijah's ministry. He is the angel who will prepare the way for the coming of the Lord. *'See, I will send my messenger, who will prepare the way before me'* (Malachi 3:1). Malachi describes the End Time as a time of dividing, when everyone will be able to distinguish between the righteous and the wicked, between the one who serves God and the one who does not serve him.

There is a connection between the parable of the good seed and the weeds, and Malachi's description of the End Time. When the separation has taken place, there are only two kinds of people: one group of people will shine like the sun in the kingdom of their Father (Matthew 13:43); the other group are those who are stumbling-blocks and who commit lawlessness (13:41).

But what about the middle group of mankind? Through separation, they have gone in two different directions: they have either become children of the kingdom, shining with God's glory, or they have become children of the evil one, who cause sin.

Malachi sees the same division happening before the great and dreadful day of the Lord comes. He sees the day coming that will burn like a furnace, with the whole world in it as in a smelting-furnace; but he also sees a redeemed people over whom the Sun of righteousness rises (Malachi 4:1–3). They leap like calves released from the stall. The others, however, Malachi sees as being trampled as on a threshing-floor, and as ashes under the soles of our feet. When the time of Jesus' coming arrives, a separation will already have taken place, and according to Malachi, the instrument for it is the prophet Elijah.

Jesus says in the parable that it is angels, messengers, who will separate the wheat from the weeds. The Elijah ministry is a ministry of messengers, an angelic mission, which will bring about the separation in the End Time.

When Jesus comes, then the definitive separation will occur on a particular day, the day that is also called the day of harvest. There are two harvests, both ready to be reaped, according to Revelation 14:14–20, and the Elijah ministry is the instrument of the step-by-step separation of the two harvests.

The harvest-time

The separation has a special purpose in God's plan. Just as in Elijah's time, the Lord today desires that the two alternatives should be clearly contrasted, so that it will be easy for people to choose between them. The separation in the End Time will create a situation where there is a choice; after that there comes the time of harvest. But until then, the living Church must crystallise itself as a clearly distinguished alternative, so that secularised mankind will have no difficulty in seeing the choice that exists between the kingdom of darkness and the kingdom of light.

Many Christians believe in this separation, but only as something that happens on the other side of death, and after the coming of Jesus. But God's word shows that it is a process that happens in the End Time while we are still in the world, and that the people of God take a part in the process. We become God's instruments, in an active sense, as soon as God gives the order that the time has come for the harvesters to go out and separate the wheat from the weeds; and such an order is going out now. We are living in the closing period of the age, which is called the harvest-time. Now the world is going to reap both the evil and the good that have been sown through the various ideologies.

The threshing-floor

On the threshing-floor, the chaff is separated from the wheat.

> *'His winnowing fork is in his hand, and he will clear his threshing-floor, gathering his wheat into the barn and burning up the chaff with unquenchable fire.'*
>
> (Matthew 3:12)

There is going to be an oppression, a resistance, against the people of God in the last days, described in the Bible as a *'trampling'*. All that is called holy will be blasphemed in the kingdom of Antichrist. God has a plan for the city of Jerusalem in the next age: it will be the centre of Jesus' government of peace. But there is a hatred of this plan of God's – a hatred that is of Antichrist; and for this reason *'Jerusalem will be trampled on by the Gentiles'* (Luke 21:24). *'They will trample on the holy city for 42 months'* (Revelation 11:2). In fact, all the visions that God has given us will be trampled underfoot by a world that does not understand them; but in this way, the forces of evil serve the purposes of God.

The word *'trampling'* describes what happens on the threshing-floor. During my time as a missionary in Pakistan, I saw the old method of threshing in action. They laid out the sheaves on a piece of hard ground, and oxen were made to walk about with their eyes covered up, trampling continuously on the sheaves. When this was over, everything had been crushed by the feet of the oxen. Later, on a day when a light wind was blowing, the men came with their winnowing shovels, throwing shovelfuls of the mixed grain and chaff into the air so that the wind separated them. The chaff was carried away a short distance by the wind, while the grain, being heavier, fell straight downwards.

Psalm 1 likens the wicked to chaff blown away by the wind.

The time before the coming of Jesus will be a time of crises, of pressure and of oppression. This time is needed in order that the Lord can distinguish between the chaff and the wheat. Therefore, our visions too will encounter continual misunderstanding; and those that we most clearly recognise as revealed to us by the Lord, will meet with the strongest resistance. The oppression from the spiritual forces of evil in the heavenly places is increasing, and the people of God in the End Time feel as if they are living in a tunnel. But the evil forces ultimately serve the purposes of God by being an instrument on the threshing-floor, like the oxen walking round and round with their eyes covered.

The wine-press of wrath

In the last times, the Lord will trample the wine-press of his wrath. He tramples down all rebellion, all that sets itself up against the knowledge of God. He tramples down ideologies and systems of thought that are of Antichrist (Isaiah 63:1–6). Isaiah describes the final judgment over the false and the true Israel (Isaiah 66:1–7). The Lord is inclined to be rough in his treatment of that which displeases him. There is much in our lives and in our churches that does not glorify the Lord, things that provoke him to anger: all this he will trample down. Before he tramples the world in the wine-press of his wrath, the judgment of the wine-press begins over God's house.

Both the threshing-floor and the wine-press are instruments for the time when the harvest is ripe.

The goldsmith's crucible

One method that the Lord is going to use in the last days, in order to bring about separation, is to allow his people to go through heat and fire. We shall end up in the goldsmith's crucible so that the dross can be separated from the gold. The Elijah ministry is the instrument for bringing this crucible into existence, so that the gold can be separated from the dross before Jesus comes (Malachi 3:1–4). The Lord will be like a refiner's fire, and he will sit and purify the Levites, so that they can bring offerings in righteousness. The gold here stands for a righteous economy, while the dross stands for economic unrighteousness and any mixing together with the world's unrighteous economic system. It is going to be our economy that ends up in the crucible.

In the time before the coming of Jesus, oppression from the kingdom of Antichrist will be so strong that there will be a fire which the Lord will use to transform us into people of gold, people who can be allowed into the city of gold, the new Jerusalem. Before the kingdom of God can come on earth, everything that belongs to the kingdom of darkness must be wiped out and destroyed. This process begins with the people of God. Apart from the economy, everything that we have done, or do, must go into the crucible.

A group of worship leaders had agreed to lead the worship at a particular conference. They found it more than usually difficult to choose the right songs. All the words of songs are tested in the light of God, and their choice of songs and service for God in worship-leading were in the crucible. They felt the Lord was saying that even if there was only a small particle of gold remaining, it would be better to make use of that than to use anything that would not be pleasing to the Lord.

Freedom from compromise in the Elijah ministry

To be an instrument of separation requires a freedom from compromise and a firm reliability. The Lord said to Ezekiel:

> *'I will make you as unyielding and hardened as they are. I will make your forehead like the hardest stone, harder than*

> *flint. Do not be afraid of them or terrified by them, though*
> *they are a rebellious house.'*   (Ezekiel 3:8–9)

This hardness of which the Lord speaks is not lack of love. Ezekiel was full of love for his people; without love, he could never have been the bearer of all his brilliant visions of the future, in which he saw the restoration of his people. The hardness that the Lord speaks about is a firmness, a fearlessness and a freedom from compromise, that which made both Elijah and John the Baptist go out into the desert and separate themselves from the Antichrist system of their times. Elijah came into confrontation with the Antichrist system, and challenged Ahab. John the Baptist confronted an unrighteous society with a sharp call to repentance (Luke 3:4–14).

This firmness was also found in Paul, when he withstood the false brothers who wanted to bring the Judaistic, legalistic spirit into the Galatian church (Galatians 2:4–5). Paul did not yield to them for a moment; he entered into a heated exchange of words with them, so there was a sharp division between them (Acts 15:2). Paul was not afraid of causing a rift by standing firmly against any attempt at a religious compromise.

In the process that leads to a division between the true Church that is the Bride of Christ, and the false church; between God's kingdom and that of Antichrist, the Lord comes and uses his people who are willing to carry out the Elijah ministry of separation. For this reason, we should not be afraid of bringing about confrontations that lead to the carrying out of God's deepest purposes.

The double-edged sword that separates

Out of the mouth of the glorified Christ there went a sharp double-edged sword (Revelation 1:16; 2:12, 16). God's word is the sharp double-edged sword that divides in this way (Hebrews 4:12).

It is the attitude of people for or against the word of God that brings about the great division between the true and the false church. Once when we were having a day of prayer, we received this message: 'I, the Lord, have drawn my sword, and through you I will carry out the ministry of the sword in separation. I will use the sword against all the political parties in this land. I will use the sword against my Church, and against your own hearts. A sword will even penetrate to your soul. The sword will create confusion, but it will cause the separation that I the Lord desire to make in your life, in the Church and in this land.'

God's message always has a dividing effect. Hebrews 4 describes how the message of God reached Israel that they should go into the promised land, where they would enter into rest and cease from their wanderings in the desert. But this welcome message led to a division. A number of them believed the word, but others were disobedient. Some became challenging examples of overcoming faith; I am thinking of Joshua and Caleb. Most of them became examples of disobedience as a warning to us. Some entered into God's rest, and found rest from their works. Others continued with their own works and went their own ways. In this way, the good news caused a separation.

The message of good news, *'Believe in the Lord Jesus, and you will be saved'* divides mankind into those that believe and are saved, and those who do not believe. It is the same with those truths that come through the renewal in these times. When the Lord brings out the message of the Holy Spirit and the gifts of the Spirit, the Church is divided between those who receive and those who say no. When those who receive the gifts of the Spirit continue in love and service to one another, the Body of Christ is built up as a living organism, but at the same time the pressure increases on the organisational, bureaucratic church. When, for example, I teach in a church about walking in faith, the opposite attitude crystallises in those who do not want to walk in faith. When I teach about the worshipping church, I find that in contrast to the worshipping believers, there are those who say 'no' to worshipping. Teaching about the prophetic Church causes a collision with the frightened church.

If you want to be a member of the Bride-Church, you will

have to accept the authority of the double-edged sword that separates between soul and spirit, joints and marrow, and judges the thoughts and attitudes of the heart.

Chapter 11

Elisha's Ministry of Reigning

Elisha became a prophet in the place of Elijah (1 Kings 19:16). He had a deep desire to receive a double portion of Elijah's spirit (2 Kings 2:9). He had asked for a hard thing, and could only get it on one condition: that he had his eyes on Elijah at the moment when Elijah was taken up to heaven by a chariot of fire. Elisha did so, and Elijah's mantle fell to him, as the sign that he was taking over Elijah's task. The equipment and the commissioning for the task came from the Lord, but they could also be transmitted from one person to another by a unique act of the Holy Spirit. The experience and the ministry of Elijah in prophecy were handed over to Elisha through the teacher-pupil relationship that existed between the two men. In these times, a mantle can fall to a person through, for example, laying-on of hands.

The younger prophets gave testimony that the spirit of Elijah was truly resting on Elisha (2 Kings 2:15). Elijah was like an army for Israel: *'My father! My father! The chariots and horsemen of Israel!'* (2:12). When it came to describing Elisha's ministry, the same words were used by the king of Israel, showing that Elisha was truly continuing the acts of Elijah (2 Kings 13:14).

What happened to Elisha helps to clarify for us the mysterious prophecy that Elijah will come back. Elijah came back through Elisha. A person can continue to carry out the task of another person, through the Lord passing on to him a similar anointing in the Holy Spirit.

The mantle of Elijah also fell upon John the Baptist, who came in the spirit and power of Elijah.

In the End Time, the mantle of Elijah will fall upon many people, all carrying on the same ministry as Elijah himself.

Elijah used his spiritual authority in a ministry of restoration, while that which characterises Elisha's ministry is ruling with the Lord.

Elijah was the prophet who started his ministry when all the prophets had been killed by Jezebel. King Ahab looked upon him as an enemy, as the one who caused trouble in Israel. Through his ministry of restoration, many things changed during his lifetime. Elisha continued Elijah's ministry on a new level as a respected adviser to kings, and is a picture of the Church reigning with Christ.

The Church reaches a position of reigning with Christ only in the next age, but even in this age we are in training for Kingdom government. It is through the wisdom of the Lord that kings reign and rulers decree justice. When the prophets are in his presence, they receive insight and wisdom so that they can warn and advise leaders of nations. To reign with Christ is to see his miracle-power released, to solve problems on a personal and national level, where there are no other human solutions.

Elisha's prophetic ministry as a foretaste of the kingdom of peace

Even now we have tasted the powers of the age to come, and therefore we can demonstrate the power that belongs to the kingdom of God. Elisha demonstrated in his time, powers that belong to the coming kingdom of peace.

1. Elisha and the widow, and the miracle of the flowing oil (2 Kings 4:1–7). God performed a miracle through Elisha that released the Lord's unlimited resources to set a widow and her family free from debt. The creditors had come and threatened to take her two sons as slaves. All her vessels were miraculously filled with oil, and Elisha told her to sell the oil, pay her debts and save her sons from slavery.

The spirit of the Babylonian society causes people to live

beyond their means and accept permanent debt. The year of jubilee was instituted with its proclamation of freedom from all debts to God and to men. You need to be free from debt on the day when Antichrist proclaims his control over all who buy and sell. The prophetic Church is not to live according to the rules of the economy of this present age, accepting the slavery of Babylon. We are to reign with Christ in an Elisha-anointing, and by this means we are to be used by God for economic miracles that will set people free from debts and nations free from being dependent on the financial institutions of the New World Order.

2. The Shunammite's son, raised from the dead (2 Kings 4:8–37). The bones of Elisha were so charged with the power of life that even after his death a dead man, buried in Elisha's grave, came to life and stood up on his feet as soon as his body touched Elisha's bones (2 Kings 13:20–21).

Jesus told his disciples, *'As you go, preach this message, "The kingdom of heaven is near." Heal the sick, raise the dead'* (Matthew 10:7–8). The kingdom of darkness is a kingdom of death, and death is manifested in many ways in that kingdom through accident, terminal illness, attempted suicide, abortion, AIDS, and so on. Eternal life wins the victory over death. The resurrection power is demonstrated through the prophetic church. AIDS sufferers are healed; covenants with death are broken; the abortion rate goes down; less people commit suicide. Symbols of death disappear when artists come to the Lord; the source of their creativity is no longer the culture of the kingdom of death, but the Hosanna culture. In my own church, for seven years no member died and we had no funerals. Instead, we had many weddings in the church and many new-born children were dedicated to the Lord.

3. Elisha was used by God to bring healing to land that was unproductive and to food that was poisonous (2 Kings 2:19–22; 4:38–41). He went to the spring in Jericho and threw salt into it, saying: *'This is what the Lord says: "I have healed this water. Never again will it cause death or make the land unproductive."'* The Elijah ministry operates on a level of faith that expects God's mighty deeds to be revealed in the creation through healing.

The Scripture says: *'The earth is defiled by its people; they have disobeyed the laws, violated the statutes and broken the everlasting covenant. Therefore a curse consumes the earth'* (Isaiah 24:5–6). The prophets in the Bible felt compassion when there had been no rain in the land, when people were starving, when the harvest was destroyed by locusts and when they were seeking the Lord to know why drought, famine and disaster had come. The Lord promised: *'I will forgive their sin and heal their land.'* The scientists and politicians are without effective solutions to the environment problems of today. The Lord will send prophets and intercessors, with the Elijah anointing upon them, to the ecological catastrophe areas of the world with a message of repentance that will bring healing to the land if it is received and acted upon. The one who has been given authority to shut heaven, so that there is no rain, also has authority to open heaven so that rain falls once more. So too the one who has authority to turn water into blood, also has authority to turn contaminated water into drinking water.

Where are the Elishas of today, who will seek the Lord for the healing of polluted lakes and rivers, and for action that will save the rain forests, the 'green lungs of the earth'? Jesus is coming back with healing for the holes in the ozone layer at the North and South Poles. When he comes, the deserts will bloom, the Dead Sea will be filled with fish, and harmony will come to destructive weather-patterns.

The Gospel is a proclamation of hope for the whole of creation. The Lord has the answers on how the creation will be freed from pollution and from destruction of the environment, and this will be demonstrated through the prophetic Church as a foretaste of the coming Kingdom.

4. The miracle of the loaves (2 Kings 4:42–44). Twenty small loaves were sufficient for a hundred men, and still there were pieces left over. It was a miracle of the same kind as Jesus did when he blessed the five loaves and the two small fish, so that they became sufficient for thousands of people. This kind of miracle belongs to the Kingdom of God, and will be shown in action when Antichrist tries to control the buying and selling of food in the End Time. The Lord will raise up a

Joseph ministry. Joseph interpreted the prophetic dreams that God gave to Pharaoh to save the nation in a time of famine. He was released from prison and was given the keys to all the storehouses in Egypt. During the seven good years, Joseph filled the storehouses with grain, so that he was able to save the people from starvation during the seven years of famine that came over all the earth. The Lord has given an End Time calling to farmers and businessmen: 'Feed my people in a time of great need.'

Why did John see God's people as a woman clothed with the dream of Joseph – the sun, moon and stars (Revelation 12:1)? I believe that she was dressed in Joseph's dream because in the End Time the Joseph ministry will be pre-eminent among God's people. *'The woman fled into the desert to a place prepared for her by God, where she might be taken care of for 1,260 days'* (Revelation 12:6).

5. Naaman, the general of the Aramean army, was healed of leprosy (2 Kings 5:1–27). This is an example of a fulfilment of the prophecy in Isaiah 2, that the nations will stream to the house of the Lord to get help. There will be evangelisation through the attraction of God's glory, just as the rumour of Elisha's works of power reached the pagan people of his time. Elisha said, *'Make the man come to me and he will know that there is a prophet in Israel'* (2 Kings 5:8). The Lord has changed into a higher gear to disciple the nations, and through us he wants to reach the heads of states and the most influential leaders in the Gentile nations and demonstrate his healing power.

6. The punishment of Gehazi (2 Kings 5:20–27). Gehazi was in line to be the next one to receive the mantle of Elijah, but greed filled his heart and with lies and deceit he went after a reward from Naaman. Elisha exposed him, and he was judged with the leprosy of Naaman; immediately he became a leper, white as snow. The more mightily the presence of the Lord is manifested, the more quickly he will be ready to punish disobedience. The Lord's reign in the nations also includes the rod of iron, which was the weapon that a shepherd used to defend his sheep from the wild beasts. Jesus said to the overcomers of Thyatira:

> *'To him who overcomes and does my will to the end, I will give authority over the nations – "He will rule them with an iron sceptre; he will dash them to pieces like pottery" just as I have received authority from my Father.'*
>
> (Revelation 2:26–27)

The Lord is slow to anger, and he gives a prolonged time of grace to sinners, but when he is working at the level of God's kingdom establishing itself in nations, we are on super-holy ground, and he will not tolerate greed and deceit in the life of one of his ambassadors; he delivers swift punishment.

7. Elisha and the lost axe-head (2 Kings 6:1–7). Even everyday problems are solved by the power of God's kingdom. Reigning with Christ means solving all the problems we meet, in the spirit and power of God's kingdom. This incident means that even the laws of nature can become our obedient servants, as the law of gravity in this case. When carpenters and construction workers have fresh testimonies of the Lord's intervention in daily life, the kingdom of heaven is at hand.

All the signs of God's kingdom in the life of Elisha belong together in the kingdom of peace. These signs of the kingdom will also be present in the restored Church, reigning with Christ through times of hardship, just as they will also be in the next age.

Chapter 12

Liberated Areas

God has places that are in a special sense under his protection. God's kingdom concerns both people and localities. Through Elisha, we can see how the places where he lived were under this special protection of God.

To enable us to understand Jesus' work of reconciliation, the task of the Church in this age and our hope for the future in the age to come, God has supplied us with spiritual realities in the form of pictures and illustrations. One such picture is that of the city of refuge, as given in the Old Testament.

1. The city of refuge was a place that the Lord himself would designate

'He is to flee to a place I will designate' (Exodus 21:13). When Israel came into the promised land, the Lord would appoint places of refuge. The Lord wants to show you both the place and the house or flat where you should be living. In the kingdom of peace, God's will will be done on earth, right down to the smallest detail. In the place that is not under God's protection, everyone does exactly as he wants, and no one asks the Lord where he should live.

2. The city of refuge was a place to which a person might flee from the avenger of blood

Moses received instructions to choose six towns to which a person being pursued could flee for refuge (Numbers 35:9–15).

The spiritual application is that the city of refuge is a place to which we can flee to escape from God's wrath, but also from the wrath of Satan or Antichrist. The city of refuge becomes, in the last stage of the life of the Church in this age, a place where we can take refuge from persecution by Antichrist.

The picture of the city of refuge is fulfilled most completely in Christ. *'We who have fled to take hold of the hope offered to us may be greatly encouraged'* (Hebrews 6:18–20). *'In you, O Lord, I have taken refuge'* (Psalm 31:1–4). The city of refuge is also fulfilled in the new Jerusalem, a city that is protected by high walls, with angels on guard at the gates, and a careful description of all that must remain outside (Revelation 21:8, 21:27). But that which is fulfilled in Christ is also fulfilled in his Church, so that the Church becomes an illustration of the city of refuge.

3. The roads leading to the cities of refuge should be kept in good order

It should be made easy for the refugee to flee there (Deuteronomy 19:1–12).

4. The one who flees to the city of refuge must put his case before the elders

When he has put his case to the elders, the assembly should decide the matter (Joshua 20:1–9). In order for a home, a church or a community to be a city of refuge, there must be 'elders' there, a leadership given by the Lord. Spiritual leaders act as shields, as a protection for the people (Psalm 47:9). The one who comes as a refugee must submit to the leadership that the Lord has appointed. Rebellion is an attribute of the kingdom of darkness; God cannot protect rebellion. His kingdom is one of order.

5. A royal priesthood and a spiritual geography

God's own people were to be a kingdom of priests; in practice, this meant that the priests and Levites were allotted 48 towns throughout the whole of Israel, and out of these, six were at the same time, to be cities of refuge (Joshua 21). These were:

Hebron, Shechem, and Kedesh in Galilee; and east of the Jordan, Bezer, Ramoth Gilead and Golan. Looking at the positions of these towns marked on the map, it is clear that Israel had a spiritual geography.

Has our own country also a spiritual geography? Some areas have perhaps been places of particular awakening, with many people saved and many churches, whereas other areas are spiritually harder and more difficult. This has certainly been our experience in Sweden.

God's purposes in local awakenings in the past have been the restoring of his kingdom, a conquest of the land, a kingdom of priests, a spiritual geography, all characteristics of his purposes with Israel. But in most Western countries God's purposes have not been fully upheld, because the Christians in each locality have been divided among different churches. As long as we remain fragmented in this way, we cannot see the full vision. A Church bound by denominational thinking cannot see the whole vision for its area.

Places of refuge, and places under God's curse

In order to understand a country's spiritual geography, we must be conscious that there are some places under God's special protection, and that there are other places under God's judgment.

Places of refuge

Bethel. This was the place to which Jacob fled from the vengeance threatened by his brother Esau. During the night, as he slept with a stone as his pillow, he had a dream in which he saw heaven opened and angels going up and down on a ladder. When he awoke, he said: *'How awesome is this place! This is none other than the house of God; this is the gate of heaven'* (Genesis 28:17).

Zoar. When Lot had to flee from Sodom, he appealed to the angels to spare the small town of Zoar, and the angel promised that the town would be protected: *'I will not overthrow the town you speak of'* (Genesis 19:19–22). Zoar means 'small'. In Sodom, the homosexual life-style had taken over, so that there was an attempt at homosexual assault on the angels. If something like this happens, and the homosexual life-style becomes accepted, it will affect larger places and cities. It will then be necessary for us to seek out the small places in the country that have not yet been infected with the spirit of Sodom.

Jerusalem. *'Jerusalem will be holy'* (Joel 3:17).

Places under God's judgment and curse

Sodom. Lot said to his sons-in-law: *'Hurry and get out of this place, because the Lord is about to destroy the city!'* (Genesis 19:14).

Jericho. Jericho was wiped out and cursed (Joshua 6:26; 1 Kings 16:34).

In the last days, both these opposite poles will be present. We have the city of Antichrist, which the Bible calls Babylon, which has become a haunt for every evil spirit. The warning to God's people is to come out of her (Revelation 18:1–4). We are coming to see more and more of this demonic community; but there is the opposite pole also. There is a place prepared by God, far from the serpent's reach, a place where the people of God can flee from the avenger of blood and where they can be cared for and protected (Revelation 12:6; 12:14).

'Enter your rooms and shut the doors behind you; hide yourselves for a little while until his wrath has passed by.'
(Isaiah 26:20–21)

We need to find out where these cities of refuge are, where God's people will be able to live safely during the time of the wrath of Antichrist.

In the first place we need to learn how to make our own homes become places of refuge. When the wrath of God went out over Egypt and the angel of death caused the firstborn of every family to die, there were 'rooms' to enter that were protected from the wrath. These were the households that were under the protection of the blood, because the father of the house had put the blood of the lamb on the top and sides of the door-frame.

Secondly, we need to learn how the Church and the places where we hold services and meetings can become liberated areas. Christian fellowships in residential areas need to learn God's laws and principles for cities of refuge. In the last days it will be necessary to have places of refuge during the period of persecution by Antichrist.

I have sought the Lord in prayer and asked about the End Time: 'Lord, you provided six cities of refuge in Israel, so that someone who was being pursued by the avenger of blood would be able to save his life by fleeing there. How are you going to provide refuge for your people in the End Time, Lord, when we shall have to face Antichrist, the worst avenger of blood the world has ever seen? You provided six cities of refuge for one nation; what are you going to provide for a whole world? We need six nations or regions in the world as free zones in the end time.'

I believe these nations will be liberated through prayer warfare. By means of a mighty harvest, such areas will be populated with faithful disciples of Jesus; and a condition for such a nation to become a nation of refuge will be that it will have to go through a mini-tribulation before the rest of the world comes to face the full tribulation. Tribulation comes for the purpose of cleansing a nation and making it ready for the kingdom. It is only when a nation goes through the storm, the fire and the shaking that it can become a nation of refuge. If you ask for your nation to become a place of refuge, therefore, I believe you are asking for a mini-tribulation to cleanse your land.

The city of refuge as illustrated in Elisha's prophetic ministry

Where Elisha lived, there were manifestations of God's kingdom that belong with the concept of a city of refuge. While Elijah was alive, he had to flee from deadly enemies, hiding himself and wandering in the desert. The prophets had to hide in caves. But through Elijah's ministry of restoration, the situation was so completely altered that Elisha could live in his

own house and have a school of prophets in the neighbourhood. Through Elisha, we learn how a restored Church works
in a state of ruling with Christ.

The ministry of prophetic information about the enemy's plans

Everything that the enemy planned in secret conferences
became known to Elisha through prophetic information
(2 Kings 6:18–22). It is one of the advantages of the prophets
and friends of the Lord that they are well-informed about the
enemy's plans. In the rebellion of Antichrist against the Lord
described in Psalm 2, the leaders of the people conspire
against the Lord with the kings and rulers of the earth. The
Lord's army in the End Time needs a keen intelligence service
like that of Elisha. We need a ministry of prophetic information, better than all the microphones placed by a secret police
force for secret listening purposes. We need constant prophetic situation reports about the enemy's next step, so that we
can know beforehand about all the events leading to Antichrist's power take-over. If we are to face Antichrist's power
take-over, when no one will be able to buy or sell without the
mark of the beast, then we must pray that we can learn about
these things long before they happen.

The city of refuge is surrounded by an angelic army

At first Gehazi, Elisha's servant, could only see that the town
was surrounded by an enemy army who intended to put Elisha
out of action; but when Gehazi's eyes were opened, he saw
what Elisha had already seen in the spirit – that their town was
protected by an angelic army (2 Kings 6:13–17).

Paradise is guarded by angels (Genesis 3:24). The new
Jerusalem has twelve gates, with twelve angels at the gates
(Revelation 21:12). In God's protection of the city of refuge,
angels have an important function. God will command his
angels to guard us (Psalm 91:11).

The enemy is blinded

'*Strike these people with blindness*', Elisha prayed, and the
Lord blinded them (2 Kings 6:18–20). Many Christians under

the Communist governments had similar experiences. In one church, an agent of the secret police used to sit and take note of what was going on in the meetings. On particular occasions the church stationed special members around him, praying, 'Confuse his mind, make him blind, so that he does not see what is going on in the meeting.' He did not even notice that there was a foreigner who spoke in the meeting and was interpreted.

Satan is not all-powerful. When he is thrown down, there will be places that he has never looked into. When he persecutes the people of God, he will be blinded from seeing the places where they have taken refuge. *'A place prepared ... by God ... out of the serpent's reach'* (Revelation 12:6, 12:14).

In the city of refuge, there is no avenging

Elisha was able to lead the blinded enemy astray and then, when they were in the middle of Samaria, their eyes were opened. The king of Israel in Samaria wanted to kill them, but Elisha told the king to give them food and water. In the city of refuge, no one has the right to act in vengeance (2 Kings 6:20–23).

Protection from the enemy's attacks

The king of Israel blamed Elisha for the desperate famine, and determined to send a man to kill him. The man hastened to do his task, and hard on his heels came the king to see that his order was carried out. Elisha was given prophetic warning of the imminent danger, and before the executioner could reach him, he shut the door against him. The Bible does not tell us exactly what it was that suddenly happened so that the executioner stopped obeying the king's order and asked a question that betrayed his own insecurity *'Why should I wait for the Lord any longer?'* (2 Kings 6:31–33).

This incident is a parallel of what will happen to God's people in the End Time, when the Church has to go underground in the conflict with Antichrist. The dragon persecutes the woman. The serpent spews water over the woman to sweep her away, but the attack is stopped, by the earth opening up and helping the woman (Revelation 12:13–16).

> *'When the enemy shall come in like a flood, the spirit of the Lord shall lift up a standard against him.'*
>
> (Isaiah 59:19, KJV)

Your kingdom come!

The kingdom of God is historical and geographical, not merely spiritual. When you pray *'Your kingdom come'*, you can put an address on the prayer. Your kingdom come to X-street! One day, the glory of God will fill the whole earth, but he can do it in advance, as he did in the upper room at Pentecost.

What answer do we get when we pray *'Your kingdom come'*?

1. The kingdom comes in complete fulfilment through a dramatic intervention in history, when Jesus Christ comes back as king of the whole earth.
2. The kingdom comes here and now as a foretaste, a prophecy, a sample on a small scale of what will happen later on a large scale.

The kingdom of God here and now is in constant conflict. The kingdom is restored in the enemy's territory, and the whole world is under the control of the evil one. We are here as the Lord's guerrilla army; we occupy small areas and seek to hold these and to expand the battlefield until Jesus comes. God's kingdom in this age is always under attack from the enemy.

God's kingdom is an area

Where Jesus is, there is the kingdom of God. When Jesus rode into Jerusalem, he was met with rejoicing. The people shouted *'Hosanna!'* and greeted him with the words, *'Blessed is the coming kingdom of our father David!'* (Mark 11:10). When they saw Jesus, they saw David's kingdom coming. When Jesus is present among us, there is the kingdom of God; Jesus is present with his Body.

Where God's will is done on earth. *'Your will be done on earth as it is in heaven.'* In the rest of the world, lawlessness reigns, rebellion against the ten commandments, against God's Word, against the order of creation, against all that is called holy.

Those who win the victory in the closing stage of this age are those who obey God's commandments and hold to the testimony of Jesus (Revelation 12:17). There are going to be places where people obey God's commandments, and there are also going to be places where complete lawlessness prevails. This separation will take place all the more when the people of God take up the call in earnest and come out of the community of Antichrist (Revelation 18:4).

Where people and places are cleansed by the blood of Jesus (Zechariah 13:1). A fountain will be opened to cleanse the inhabitants of Jerusalem from their sin and impurity. On that day, the Lord will remove the spirit of impurity from the land. Daniel prayed a prayer as the representative of his people, which cleansed the people from the curse that was on them, and from God's wrath (Daniel 9). In Egypt, judgment fell on the innocent lamb, and its blood was put on the door-frame, so that the house would be protected when the judgment went out over Egypt (Exodus 12).

An area that is no longer under the wrath of God. In the End Time, the whole earth will be struck by the wrath of God, but even then there will be hiding-places, rooms, where it will be possible to hide from the wrath of God (Isaiah 26:20). *'The earth will disclose the blood shed upon her; she will conceal her slain no longer'* (Isaiah 26:21). The ground is defiled with murder, abortion, and acts of violence. The Lord in the day of his wrath will carry out a spring-cleaning, so that the world can go into the kingdom of peace; but this spring-cleaning can and will begin in advance with the Church of God (1 Peter 4:17–18).

Today God's wrath is directed against the Church – against everything that the Lord has not planned. *'Every plant that my heavenly Father has not planted will be pulled up by the roots'* (Matthew 15:13). There is much in our lives and in the Church that grows, though the Lord never planted it. That sort of thing must be struck down now, in order that there can be a protected area when God's wrath comes on the whole earth.

Before the second world war, it happened in a town in Germany that a crowd of people incited by hatred of the Jews

141

let their hatred loose over a whole Jewish quarter of the town, where there was a synagogue. They burnt down and destroyed everything, so that the whole of the Jewish quarter was levelled to the ground. Later came the last phase of the war, when the British bombed the town, and many houses in the neighbourhood where the synagogue had stood, were burning. The only place that was safe for people to go to escape the fire was the burnt-down Jewish quarter, where there was nothing left to burn.

The whole earth filled with God's glory

The final objective is that the whole earth should be filled with the glory of God. *'They will neither harm nor destroy on all my holy mountain, for the earth will be full of the knowledge of the Lord as the waters cover the sea'* (Isaiah 11:9).

At Pentecost both the house and the people in it were filled with the glory of God. For God it is just as important to fill you with the Holy Spirit as to fill your house.

The ground can be cursed for our sakes and can also be blessed for our sakes. *'You will be blessed in the city and blessed in the country'* (Deuteronomy 28:3). *'You will be cursed in the city and cursed in the country'* (28:16).

If a Church is blessed by the Lord, the town or neighbourhood is also blessed; and the contrary is true likewise.

Chapter 13

John the Baptist –
In the Spirit of Elijah

The Elijah ministry has its clearest historical manifestation in John the Baptist. John had the task of preparing the way for Jesus at his first coming. We, who have the task of preparing the way for Messiah at his second coming, have much to learn from the Elijah ministry of John.

John had a special prophetic mission for the transition period between two ages of history, and he started to declare this openly some months before Jesus began his ministry. The age of the law came to an end and the age of grace began when Jesus came. The prophetic Church has a similar special prophetic mission in the transition between two ages. John's mission was to make ready a people prepared for the Lord (Luke 1:17); to prepare people to receive Jesus and his preaching. This time too, the Lord seeks to have a well-prepared people.

The task of Zechariah in forming John for his Elijah ministry

Zechariah was a priest belonging to the eighth division out of the twenty-four divisions of priests who served in the temple. During his time of duty, he received a revelation in the form of an angel of the Lord appearing to him, standing at the right side of the altar of incense. Zechariah had prayed for a child after a long childless marriage, and now came the angel with a message that his prayer was answered and that his wife Elizabeth would bear a son, who would be like Elijah in his power

143

and in his mission. The angel gave a prophetic description of the calling of John and of his life's task, and made Zechariah responsible for bringing John up to be someone radically different from what Zechariah had been. If the angel had not given these instructions, John would simply have become another priest in the eighth division like his father. As it was, he became a prophet in the desert; instead of becoming a traditional priest, he became a Nazirite.

The description of John the Baptist's calling

1. *'He will be great in the sight of the Lord.'* The mission given to John was of enormous importance for the coming of God's kingdom to the world. The greatness of this mission was not to be measured by the world's standards in might, or official position, or status symbols, but by reference to Jesus. John received the testimony that no one born of woman was greater than he; what made him great was that he was sent by God into a prophetic ministry at the right appointed time. He was great, too, in his humility; he was able to be glad when he saw Jesus' influence growing while his own was decreasing.

2. *'He is never to take wine or other fermented drink.'* Abstaining from wine was one of the marks of the Nazirite vow. A Nazirite was one who was separated and consecrated to the Lord. Some of them were dedicated as Nazirites for the whole of their lives, and in that case the abstinence from drink began from the moment of birth. Nazirites had to be separated from the rest of mankind (Numbers 6). That they should not get drunk depended on the Lord wanting to govern their thoughts and consciences in every way, so that they could live in prophetic watchfulness.

Before the coming of Jesus there were many warnings about being sober. Excess and drunkenness are things that weigh down people's hearts (Luke 21:34).

The kingdom of darkness strives, through pressure on the mind and the spirit, to neutralise, lead astray, and smooth down strong personalities, so that they become apathetic about what is happening around them. In that way they can be more easily manipulated, and there will be no risk of their recognising the difference between lies and truth. 'Drunkenness' is not only from alcohol, but also from, for example, excessive television watching or a consuming interest in sport. Drugs, pornography, rock music, sport and other forms of entertainment on TV, all work together to pacify and neutralise nations, particularly young people. They create politically apathetic personalities, all in accordance with a deliberate plan from the kingdom of darkness.'

3. **'Filled with the Holy Spirit even from birth.'** The angel said to Zechariah, *'He will be filled with the Holy Spirit even from birth'* (Luke 1:15). When the pregnant Elizabeth heard the greeting from the mother of Jesus, the baby leaped in her womb, and she was filled with the Holy Spirit (Luke 1:40–41). In this way, John was filled with the Spirit from birth.

The more and the longer a personality is controlled by the Holy Spirit, the wider becomes his usefulness as an instrument. Some articles, says Paul, are for noble purposes and some for ignoble.

> *'If a man cleanses himself from the latter, he will be an instrument for noble purposes, made holy, useful to the Master and prepared to do any good work. Flee the evil desires of youth.'* (2 Timothy 2:21–22)

A person who gives parts of his life to the influence of the kingdom of darkness does not, it is true, limit his eternal salvation, but he does limit his usefulness for the Lord's purpose. The Lord will one day require a body of people in whose mouth no lie can be found, and who have not defiled themselves sexually (Revelation 14:4–5). A special mission demands also a special holiness.

When Hannah asked the Lord for a son, she gave him to the Lord for all the days of his life, and Samuel was brought before the Lord to stay there for ever (1 Samuel 1:11, 22, 28). In order for such a dedication to be made, the parents need to be committed to it from childhood; that is why Zechariah and Elizabeth were told of John's calling right from the very beginning.

The prophetic word for John's ministry

John was to be a joy and delight to Zechariah, and many people would rejoice because of his birth; he would bring many of the people of Israel back to the Lord their God.

> *'And he will go on before the Lord, in the spirit and power of Elijah, to turn the hearts of the fathers to their children and the disobedient to the wisdom of the righteous – to make ready a people prepared for the Lord.'*
>
> (Luke 1:14–17)

It would be thirty years before this prophecy was fulfilled; in God's secret armoury of weapons, there are many such prophetic descriptions of the calling of particular persons. This is a mark of the last days, which are to be a prophetic time. Many will go about with a secret prophetic testimony within them of a calling, which has not yet been fulfilled, but meanwhile they are preparing themselves for it. The prophetic Church becomes a reality as many people dare to go all out for what the Lord has called them to, and to belong together in preparing for Jesus' coming to earth.

Prepare the way for the Lord in the desert!

A way was to be prepared for the Lord in the desert. The fulfilment of John's prophetic calling lay in his going out into the desert. According to the normal custom, when he reached the age of thirty he should have become a priest in the eighth division, like his father. But the Lord called him to leave the temple ministry of the priests, which was under God's wrath, and a corrupt society which was also under God's judgment. John would never have had the boldness to be a preacher of repentance, had he gone along with the national decline.

John had obeyed the call and found himself out in the desert, when all the leaders in the conspiracy of Antichrist had taken up their positions of leadership. Those who conspired against Christ were Pilate, Annas, Caiaphas, and Herod (Luke 3:1–2).

Elijah had to go out into the desert for three and a half

years; and in the End Time, the people of God will have to go out into the desert for three and a half years. There is much to indicate that Jesus, on his returning to the Mount of Olives, will first of all visit a desert community.

David went out into the desert, when the conflict with the demon-possessed Saul became too strong, and it was in the desert that he built up a kingdom of his own parallel to Saul's, so that when the time was ripe, he was ready to take over and become king of all Israel.

The Church is going to be issued with a call to come out of the community dominated by Antichrist (Revelation 18:4; 2 Corinthians 6:17). For this reason, the prophetic Church must vigilantly follow the development of this community, and watch for the moment when it steps over the anti-Christian boundary line and God's judgment upon it becomes definitive. The angels called on Lot to flee from Sodom when the homosexual community there overstepped the boundary. Noah was called to prepare for escape from a world that was coming under the wrath of God.

When lawlessness oversteps the limit set by God, when the community becomes thoroughly demonic, when the community has lost its respect for man's life and for unborn life, when it demands a loyalty from its citizens of a kind that should only be given to God, when the community demands that its members worship false gods: these are some of the signs that mark the boundary line. These were the reasons for Israel leaving Egypt, for Daniel and his friends separating themselves from the community of Babylon, and for the first Christians refusing to worship Caesar.

Journeyings in the desert

During the months before Jesus began his first ministry, a spiritual harvest was taking place. Crowds of people went out into the desert to meet John.

> 'The whole Judean countryside and all the people of Jerusalem went out to him. Confessing their sins, they were baptised by him in the Jordan River.'   (Mark 1:5)

'From the days of John the Baptist until now, the kingdom of heaven has been forcefully advancing, and forceful men lay hold of it.' (Matthew 11:12)

People stormed into the kingdom of God.

By going out into the desert, John had made himself into something of a spiritual extremist, so that he deliberately made it more difficult for himself to reach the masses; the extremism seems to have lessened the possibilities of a general awakening among the people.

Why did the crowds go out into the desert? Jesus put the same question to the people. *'What did you go out into the desert to see?'* (Matthew 11:7). A reed swayed by the wind? No, they did not go out to see a weathervane, someone who was always adjusting himself to what the current religious world and the community expected him to say. *'What did you go out to see? A man dressed in fine clothes?'* Such signs of the welfare state are to be found elsewhere, for example in kings' palaces, Jesus said. A true awakening must include elements that cannot be found anywhere else; not in the political parties, not in the mass media.

What did you go out to see? – A prophet! Jesus gave the answer. The crowds going out to the Jordan relied on John being the only true prophetic voice, one who lived before his time, one who was free to speak the truth without being bound by any false loyalties.

When Jesus came the first time to minister on earth, he sought out this extremist movement to receive from John his initiation by baptism. This shows us where Jesus makes his choice of a home: not with the religious establishment, with the chief priests, the Sanhedrin and all those they approved of, but with the desert prophet and his disciples. This pattern is going to be repeated when the time comes for Jesus' return.

Elijah's gathering of the people of Israel at Carmel was as great a miracle as the crowds streaming out to John at the Jordan.

What in our own day has most closely resembled the awakening in the desert with John the Baptist? I do not know, but there was an experience in Sweden in 1982 which I believe was the nearest thing to it that has happened in my country. In the spring and summer of that year, in a small town in the centre of Sweden, far from the main centres of population, a church that started with only 24 members held a series of meetings. By the end of the series of meetings, in July, there were about three thousand people attending; many travelled long distances from the large cities to get there, and it began to be something like the movement that started with John. In Sweden, there is an increasing concern for spiritual things, but a decrease in the numbers attending formal church services. As people mature, they grow to accept things that are happening outside the established churches.

If the Bride-Church becomes compelled to live underground in the new situation, as will happen when Antichrist forces everyone to join his economic monopoly system, then, too, a similar awakening can arise.

Similarities between John's and Elijah's ministries

When John the Baptist appears in the desert, he is a prophetic re-appearance of Elijah on Mount Carmel, but in his ministry there are also special features that belong together with the Elijah ministry in the End Time.

Elijah called the people together on Mount Carmel, while John called them out into the desert; both of them preached in a way that caused people to repent. Elijah confronted the prophets of Baal, while John confronted the Pharisees and the Sadducees. Elijah called down fire from heaven, while John foretold the coming of one who would baptise with fire.

Elijah anointed Elisha to be a prophet in his place, while John was called to perform the initiation of Jesus into his Messianic mission.

It is part of the task of the Elijah ministry in the End Time to announce the coming of the kingdom and to point Israel to their Messiah. John announced that the kingdom was near, and when Jesus came, he showed Israel who their Saviour was: *'Look, the Lamb of God, who takes away the sin of the world!'*

Expectation of the coming of Messiah

The people were full of expectancy of the coming of the Messiah, when they went out to meet John in the desert, and this expectation of the Messiah increased through John's preaching.

> *'A man who comes after me has surpassed me because he was before me. I myself did not know him, but the reason I came baptising with water was that he might be revealed to Israel.'* (John 1:30–31)

> *'But after me will come one who is more powerful than I.'* (Matthew 3:11)

John had received a sign that would enable him to recognise Messiah. *'The man on whom you see the Spirit come down and remain is he who will baptise with the Holy Spirit'* (John 1:33). John would recognise Jesus by the anointing that came from above. We must be able, like John, to distinguish the anointing of Jesus, so that we are not deceived by the false 'Messiah' anointing that rests on Antichrist. John preached that Messiah was coming, just as we now announce that Jesus is to return. There came a day when John could say to all the people: 'Now Messiah is standing among you.'

Baptism – initiation into God's kingdom

It is a part of the Elijah ministry to anoint Messiah when he enters into his kingdom; John baptised Jesus as an initiation into the ministry of the kingdom of God. But John was also exercising the same Elijah ministry when he preached repentance and baptised people in the Jordan. His baptism was a baptism of initiation for God's kingdom.

The baptism that Jesus instructed his disciples to carry out was both a baptism into the Church and a baptism into God's kingdom. There is a risk that baptism in our day may have lost its meaning of initiating people into God's kingdom, and become simply a baptism into the Church.

When the people came to be baptised by John, he gave them instructions on practical living in the kingdom of God.

He warned the people, and particularly the Pharisees and Sadducees, not to see baptism only as an object of religious fashion and an easy method of avoiding the coming wrath. He made it clear that they must, through baptism, produce fruit in keeping with repentance (Matthew 3:7–8).

Baptism should be an initiation into a life lived in a colony of the kingdom of heaven, where people know their responsibility for one another. *'The man with two tunics should share with him who has none, and the one who has food should do the same'* (Luke 3:11).

In the kingdom of God, we are to share the supply of food and clothing among one another. When a community becomes so unrighteous that it is put under the judgment of God, the people of God must be released from their dependence on the community and instead become dependent on each other's loving gifts. God's people are beginning the reformation of the Church, and establishing an economic system in line with the kingdom of God, by sharing with one another.

When the tax collectors came to be baptised, they were told that God's kingdom, for them, meant that they should collect no more than they were required by law to collect. There are other collectors to be found in the community today, who have learnt the technique of collecting more from the state in social security payments than the law intends. Many secure social advantages for themselves. The spirit of lawlessness has made people lose respect for the community.

When the soldiers asked what they should do in order to live in the kingdom of heaven, they received the reply: *'Don't extort money and don't accuse people falsely – be content with your pay'* (Luke 3:13). Demanding one's right is fashionable. The demands of selfish interests can easily turn into force and threats. In a time when people need God's blessing on every penny, it is best not to have any money that may have been forced out of someone by threats and demands. The spirit of demanding rights, which easily taints people, does not go together with living a life of faith.

John's preaching of repentance shows that God's kingdom is practical. It has to do with our place of work, and the care we have for one another.

Is the instruction given to today's candidates for baptism anything like that of John the Baptist? There have been times in the history of the Church when instruction like that of John was given to candidates for baptism. During the third century, it was part of the instruction given to catechumens to inform them which occupations were acceptable for Christians and which were not. It was permissible for a Christian to be an officer in the Roman army, provided he was not compelled to worship the Emperor. If that happened, he should take off his uniform. To be a gladiator was not allowed.

Anyone who had an occupation or pursued a business activity that was contrary to Christian principles was not received as a candidate for baptism until he had made a promise to lay it aside. Any occupation that had to do with the worship of false gods came into this category. Each occupation had its trade-guild with its particular patron gods and festivals; and in many of these trade-guilds, astrology and magic were involved.

Before the baptism, the candidate had to make a confession of faith, and together with this verbal confession there was also a promise implying a proper moral attitude. The candidate had to separate himself from the kingdom of darkness and of Satan, which he had served up to that time, and to cross over into the kingdom of God and of Christ.

When he gave his hand to the bishop, he renounced the devil and all his ceremonies; this in particular meant anything involving the worship of false gods or devil-worship, and entertainments such as the circus, the theatre, or gladiator tournaments. All these were connected with religious festivals in honour of the gods, and included ceremonies having to do with the worship of these false deities. The candidate renounced Satan's angels, an expression of the belief that behind the heathen gods there stood demonic angels who led mankind astray.

This renunciation, and the confession of faith that followed it, were given by the Christians a status equivalent to a military oath, with which a man bound himself to live and fight as a soldier of Christ in the holy Christian army. This baptismal custom was current in the Roman Empire during the third century. It points to a view of baptism according to which baptism is an initiation into the kingdom of God, a view that needs to be recaptured by God's people in the End Time.

It is a part of the Elijah ministry to initiate men and women into living in the kingdom of God.

John in Herod's Prison

John set the life of man in the context of the kingdom of heaven, and had definite convictions about what people should do in order to prepare themselves to enter into the kingdom. John gave to Herod Antipas an invitation to repent and enter the kingdom, with the warning: *'It is not lawful for you to have your brother's wife.'* That warning was the reason for John being put in prison.

In prison, John had further opportunities to talk with Herod. If John had played his cards correctly, he might have become Herod's court chaplain, but for this to happen, he would have had to withdraw his criticism of Herod's unlawful relationship with Herodias, his brother's wife.

Herod looked on John as a righteous and holy man; he feared him, and protected him, and liked to listen to him (Mark 6:20). But as for John, his purpose was to make no concessions or compromises with the kingdom of darkness, and this was more important to him than survival.

A life's work fulfilled

When John was put in prison, his life's calling, which his father received from the angel Gabriel, was fulfilled. He had completed his prophetic task. When the goal has been reached and no new directions have been received from the Lord, it is easy to end up in doubt. In the midst of his struggle with this, John sent a message to Jesus *'Are you the one who was to come, or should we expect someone else?'* (Matthew 11:2). Behind this question there lay another one, unspoken: 'Is my mission finished, or is there still something left for me to do on earth?' John's task was in fact completed, and it was part of God's plan that John's disciples should go over to Jesus and to the churches that would be founded by the apostles. He was no longer needed as leader of a movement that would shortly be dissolved.

When a life's work is crowned with martyrdom, that is victory. The two witnesses in Revelation 11 were protected until they had fulfilled their task of testifying. Only then was the beast able to open his attack on them and to overpower and kill them (Revelation 11:7).

Jesus' testimony about John

Jesus gave John this testimonial:

> 'A prophet? Yes, I tell you, and more than a prophet ... Among those born of women there has not risen anyone greater than John the Baptist.'   (Matthew 11:9–11)

Those who are the overcomers, as described in Revelation, are recognised because they have the testimony of Jesus (Revelation 19:10; 12:17).

In this testimony of Jesus lies his prophetic word concerning a person's life, in recognising and encouraging him and declaring his love for him. Anyone who has been given this sort of recognition is going to be ready to die for Jesus.

The game of intrigue that led to John's execution

The strategic moment for Herodias to take her revenge on John the Baptist came when Herod gave a banquet on his birthday, and invited his high officials and military commanders and the leading men of Galilee.

Herodias resembles Jezebel and the great prostitute of Revelation 17 in many ways. Herodias was a power-hungry and career-seeking woman, who changed her first husband for another because the first one did not have the power or prospects necessary for her to achieve her ambitions. She seduced his brother Herod to further her political career. Like Jezebel, she was a schemer. She allowed her daughter to come in and dance seductively before Herod and his guests at the banquet, knowing well how to make use of Herod's weaker side. Herod fell for the daughter's dancing and promised under oath that the girl should have whatever she might ask. He was then trapped by this ill-considered oath. Herodias got her daughter to demand the head of John the Baptist on a platter. Herod was distressed, but his guests, the officials, soldiers and leading men had all heard him swear the oath, and because of them, and the oath, he could not refuse the demand.

The trap into which Herod fell is like the trap set by Antichrist. The Bible warns us against making promises under oath. Antichrist will succeed in making many people enter into a binding covenant with him, so that they are forced into taking part in his lawlessness by the fact that they have joined his brotherhood. It is a conspiracy of lawlessness against the Lord and his anointed one, a rebellion in which people will throw off the fetters of God's kingdom in accordance with Psalm 2.

Herodias is like the great prostitute also, in that she is drunk with the blood of the saints and of those who bore testimony to Jesus (Revelation 17:6). Is Herodias also like Jezebel when it comes to the arts of witchcraft? Was it simply a demand for revenge that made Herodias want to have John's severed head brought in on a platter? Was she possibly a Satan-worshipper? Such people make use of severed heads in their sorceries and masses. Perhaps Herodias wanted to extend her powers of sorcery through the use of this particular head?

Cause of death: beheading

Beheading as a method of capital punishment will return in the time of Antichrist (Revelation 20:4). It is a method that has almost disappeared. Saudi Arabia is one of the few remaining countries that still has public execution by beheading. The Masonic lodges have the threat of beheading in their oath; the initiate promises to have his head cut off if he reveals any of the secrets of the lodge to anyone.

Antichrist's threat comes from some of the groups that threaten beheading or else actually practise it. Then in our own day there is another method of serving up someone's head on a platter: the mass media have weapons of distorting, ridiculing, and depriving of their honour, people whom they wish to silence. In every age, the masses have sought to persecute and silence the voices of the prophets, and each age has managed to discover its own most effective way of rendering the prophetic voices ineffective.

Protection or martyrdom?

Elijah was taken up to heaven, while John was beheaded. They ended their lives in quite different ways, although they both had similar prophetic ministries. John the son of Zebedee, Jesus' disciple, lived to a great age, while Peter glorified Jesus through his martyrdom (John 21:19). James the brother of John was put to death with the sword in Jerusalem, while Peter, who at that moment was in prison, was rescued from his imprisonment by the prayers of the Church (Acts 12).

Some people glorify Jesus by their lives becoming a testimony of Jesus' power to protect them. Others glorify him by going fearlessly to their deaths for him. Of the seven churches of Asia Minor, two were specially approved, Smyrna and Philadelphia. Smyrna was the suffering church (Revelation 2:8–10). This church received a message that they should prepare for suffering and martyrdom: *'Do not be afraid of what you are about to suffer ... Be faithful, even to the point of death!'* Philadelphia was the church that was promised protection:

> *'I will also keep you from the hour of trial that is going to come upon the whole world to test those who live on the earth.'* (Revelation 3:10)

The Lord is sovereign in what he decides. Jesus himself went through the baptism of suffering. The Church will attain the fullness of Christ and will take part in all of Jesus' gifts and ministries; so there must be some in the Church who are called to suffer and to give their lives as martyrs. Martyrdom is counted as one of the gifts of grace (1 Corinthians 13:2–3).

The number of the martyrs will be completed (Revelation 6:9–11). The Church has a quota of suffering to fulfil (Colossians 1:24). The prostitute is drunk with the blood of the martyrs (Revelation 18:24; 19:2).

When the Lord pronounces judgment on the great prostitute, he claims the blood of his servants out of her hand. When Herod the king ordered the execution of James the brother of John, judgement fell on him immediately in the form of a very painful, fatal disease. Tyrants fill up the measure of their sins when they spill innocent blood. The martyrs become an instrument that the Lord uses to hasten their judgment. Those who will defeat Satan and the kingdom of darkness will not love their lives so much as to shrink from death (Revelation 12:11).

How does John the Baptist fit in with modern prosperity teaching?

He would have fitted in better if he had gradually become the pastor of the largest house-church in the Middle East. This is how his entry would have read in the Christian Dictionary of Celebrities: 'John became the leader of the Jordan Movement. He held international seminars in the desert for Christian tourist pilgrims. He prayed and received a Cadillac. Married and had three sons and three daughters. Lived to the age of 80 and was taken home quickly without any illness. Author of books: *Memories of the Desert Awakening*; *I Baptised Jesus*; *Dialogues with Herod.*'

God's blessing upon John cannot possibly be measured by the standards of this prosperity teaching. John said no to all worldly success when as a young man he went out into the desert. God's testimony of his life was the recognition he sought.

Chapter 14

Ambassadors of the Kingdom of God in Antichrist's Headquarters

We meet the Elijah ministry in the two witnesses of Revelation 11. By their acts, these two witnesses remind us of Moses and Elijah. It is prophesied of both these two men in the Bible that they will come back again: of Moses this is found in Deuteronomy 18:18: *'I will raise up for them a prophet like you* [Moses] *from among their brothers'*; and of Elijah it is found in Malachi 4:5.

Jesus was a part of the fulfilment of this prophecy: Acts 3:22–23; John 6:14, 7:40. But even if Jesus is the fulfilment of the prophecy about a prophet like Moses, Revelation 11 still points to a further fulfilment in the last days. As I said earlier in this book, the ministry of Moses and Elijah will be restored through the Church of Christ, through those members of the Church who will exercise these ministries. They can do this by taking on the same spiritual equipment, and the same authority, as Moses and Elijah.

One of the signs of the last times will be the emergence in the Church of fully mature men and women of God. Even if it turns out that there are only two people who will stand in the arena and carry out the Elijah ministry and the Moses ministry in Antichrist's headquarters, yet I believe that they will take their positions there because the Church in every part of the world will, by then, be characterised by the same ministry as that of Moses and Elijah.

Moses had a ministry of deliverance to the people of God. He said to Pharaoh: *'Let my people go, so that they can worship the Lord in the desert!'*

Elijah's was a ministry of restoration in a time of decay. His cry was: *'Restore my people!'*

I believe also that God will in the End Time give to his Church two prophetic missions: the ministry of restoration and the ministry of deliverance, and that these two ministries will bring the whole Church into fulfilment of its true role.

We have up to now had to manage with a half-completed Church, a Church still under construction. But at the time for Jesus' coming, the Church will reach its fulfilment, its completion.

> *'These [two witnesses] are the two olive trees and the two lampstands that stand before the Lord of the earth.'*
>
> (Revelation 11:4)

Zechariah was the bearer of a prophetic message to Joshua and Zerubbabel, that they were to stand in the midst of a perpetually flowing stream of the power of the Holy Spirit, in order to bring the building of the new temple to its completion. Zerubbabel was to see the capstone of the building set in place in a scene of great rejoicing, when the work was done (Zechariah 4:1–10). John reminds us of this when he sees the two witnesses. The ministries of Moses and Elijah will, in the last days, stand in the midst of a perpetually flowing stream of the anointing of the Spirit, in order to bring the building of the 'temple', the Church, to its completion.

Apostles and prophets

The Church is built on the foundation of the apostles and prophets: Ephesians 2:20. But apostles and prophets are still present in the last days of the Church's existence, when the kingdom of Antichrist collapses: *'Rejoice over her* [the judgment of Babylon], *O heaven! Rejoice, saints and apostles and prophets! God has judged her for the way she treated you'* (Revelation 18:20).

Some people believe that the two witnesses are these two ministries, functioning in the midst of the community of Antichrist. That of Moses is the one most like the ministry of an apostle; Moses was the founder of God's Church of the Old Testament, and is compared to Jesus, the apostle and high priest whom we confess (Hebrews 3:1–6). Elijah was the prophet.

It is important, in the prophetic Church, that everyone should discover his or her gift and ministry, and that those who are at present bound up in traditional roles should dare to be free, so that they can enter into apostolic and prophetic ministries. The apostles and prophets need to come together and take the initiative in battling against, and defeating, the kingdom of Antichrist.

Moses and Elijah were intercessors for their people

As men of God, both Moses and Elijah had grown into accepting the responsibility of interceding for their nation (Exodus 32:7–14). When Elijah stopped the rain, and then later prayed that it would start again, it was an answer to prayer for the nation that he did this. The two witnesses, who have key positions in the End Time, will also become intercessors for their nations. It is in the capacity of intercessors that they stand constantly in opposition to the kingdom of Antichrist. They are a plague to the inhabitants of the earth by being intercessors, who stand against the anti-Christian tendencies of the nation, and even by giving the nations an ultimatum concerning their judgment if they follow Antichrist.

This ministry of intercession, which is like the ministry of Moses and Elijah, is now growing throughout the world through a movement of intercessors, with a group in each nation setting into focus the responsibility for that nation. When this movement began in Sweden, some of us wrote a leaflet calling for intercessors for our country, using Elijah as an illustration. Here are some extracts from that leaflet:

'Elijah was the solitary man of prayer who through his intercession steered the course of a nation's history and turned a people back to God. We seek to mobilise all those who are aware of having a family relationship with Elijah, in using, like him, the weapons of prayer in both shutting and opening the gates of heaven, so as to steer the Swedish people back into the ways of God.

'Elijah prayed for a famine to come upon a rich land in order to bring the people into a right standing with God. Elijah had seen that with increasing prosperity, with full storehouses and wallets, the people were becoming bolder and bolder in their ungodliness. So he shut up the heavens by prayer. Jesus himself described what happened: *". . . In Elijah's time, when the sky was shut for three and a half years and there was a severe famine throughout the land"* (Luke 4:25). A person praying has a key of power with which he can bind situations, and another key for releasing them. He can set in motion powers that prevent things from happening, as well as those that loose them and let them go.

'The world's governments should continue to recognise what it is to have people praying for them, but also what happens when those people have to oppose a government for its ungodliness.'

Elijah held a position of power with God. He expressed his certainty about his calling when he was going to meet King Ahab: *'As the Lord Almighty lives, whom I serve'* (1 Kings 18:15). The literal meaning is 'God, before whose face I stand'. Elijah used the same words as the angel Gabriel when introducing himself: *'I am Gabriel. I stand in the presence of God'* (Luke 1:19). See also Deuteronomy 10:8: *'At that time the Lord set apart the tribe of Levi to carry the ark of the covenant of the Lord, to stand before the Lord to minister and to pronounce blessings in his name'*. The two witnesses in Revelation 11 stand in the same manner before the Lord of the earth (Revelation 11:4).

'To stand before the Lord of the earth' means that these people of God do nothing without receiving directions from the Lord. It is an attitude of readiness to serve the Lord. *'As the eyes of slaves look to the hand of their master, as the eyes of a maid look to the hand of her mistress, so our eyes look to the Lord our God, till he shows us his mercy'* (Psalm 123:2). They are the representatives of his power, with a closeness to the Lord that ensures they are kept informed of his plans, and also that they can interpret what is happening on the earth. *'To stand before the Lord'* is to have a position of power before God.

When I read a chapter in the book of Revelation about the End Time, it is not a question of speculating about the course of future events. My question is rather: 'What instruction should I give in the church, and what goals should I be aiming for, in training the people of God so that we can act together within the framework of the prophetic word?' Then the answer comes: 'Train the people of God to take responsibility for interceding for the nation, teach them to minister with spiritual authority, train them in the ministries of freeing and restoring, teach them what it means to stand before the Lord; in this way you will be bringing the church into the maturity that is needed to carry out its task in the End Time'.

The two witnesses and spiritual gifts

These two witnesses are equipped with the gift of working miracles; but they have reached a maturity and a breadth of development in the use of gifts of grace, which we are not accustomed to. They use their gifts on the national level, and right out in the open.

We generally start by using spiritual gifts in prayer group meetings. It requires more boldness to come forward and use them during a public service. But even this stage is at children's level compared with God's ultimate purposes for the use of these gifts. He wants these gifts to be used in order that his power can be shown before all the nations, that the gift of working miracles should be used when the nations make their fateful choice for or against Antichrist.

We should therefore continue encouraging the members of Christ's Body to develop, and to make bold use of, their gifts of grace so as to grow in them.

If anyone tries to harm them

> *'If anyone tries to harm them, fire comes from their mouths and devours their enemies. This is how anyone who wants to harm them must die.'* (Revelation 11:5)

This was a sign, that was also present in the life of Elijah (2 Kings 1:1–17). King Ahaziah had fallen through the lattice of his upper room in Samaria and injured himself. He wanted to know, through a spiritist medium in the service of the god Baal-Zebub, whether he would recover. The angel of the Lord sent Elijah to meet the king's messengers and ask them: *'Is it because there is no God in Israel that you are going off to consult Baal-Zebub, the god of Ekron?'*

When a king, who should have known the Lord, becomes apostate and goes after false gods, that is an act of Antichrist, and Elijah challenges this act at the command of God. In the same way, the Church will challenge all tendencies that show the spirit of Antichrist breaking out. The Church will challenge the present wave of occultism when it becomes influential in the nation.

If Ahaziah had been a pagan king and acted in ignorance, Elijah would not have been able to challenge him in the way that he did. Ahaziah sent soldiers to arrest Elijah, and twice, fire fell from heaven and consumed fifty soldiers and their captain. The third captain sent to arrest Elijah, however, had such a respect for Elijah that he pleaded for his life. At present we are not to ask for fire from heaven to consume those who oppose us; Jesus stopped his disciples when they came to him with such a proposal (Luke 9:53–55). But we cannot rule out that a time may come when God will again exercise his judgment in that kind of direct manner.

Revelation 11 deals, it is true, with a time when Antichrist is ruling on the earth. Those who are sent from Antichrist to arrest the men of God have already become lost by accepting the mark of the beast, though they continue to live. Those who exercise the ministries of Moses and Elijah are brought within the same sure protection as they enjoyed. Pharaoh's army, pursuing Moses, were drowned in the Red Sea. But this protection is present only when God's people have come out of the community of Antichrist and refused to take any part in its sins (Revelation 18:4).

When intercessors pray, God can carry out his divine judgments. Once when I was visiting a communist country, I was told how God answered the prayers of a Christian community that had long prayed that they would be given permission to build a church. They applied first for a building permit. The communist party chairman in the town said no. Then the church prayed: 'Change his mind or have him removed!' He was at once transferred and down-graded. The same thing happened to the next party chairman. Then a third chairman was appointed, and when the church's representative came, he answered him: 'You are not going to get any permission to build a church. In this town, it is I who am God. I will never give you a permit.' The church prayed: 'Change him or remove him!' Immediately afterwards, the chairman was killed in a car accident. The people in the town made the connection between this event and the fact that he had called himself God and had been so determined to stop the church from being built. The fourth chairman had great respect for the praying church, and gave them permission to build. Their prayers had continued over several years before they reached their goal, but their prayers had also become the means whereby God's judgments were visited on the enemies of his Church.

Power to strike the earth

The two witnesses have power to shut up the heavens so that rain does not fall while they are prophesying; this was Elijah's act of power. They also have power over the waters, to turn them into blood; this was Moses' sign (Revelation 11:6).

As we read the book of Revelation, we see the drama of the End Time, when God sends a series of judgments on the earth. But have we seen the context in which these judgments take place? They come through the actions of the Church, in just the same way as the judgments in Egypt came through the actions of God's servant. Judgments come first in the form of an ultimatum: Pharaoh had the opportunity to obey the Lord and repent, but he refused, so then the water, for example, was turned into blood. In the same way, a triumphant, restored Church will act in the End Time, when it is reigning with Christ, joining in taking up a strong position among the nations, standing against the spirit of Antichrist, and above all, showing itself to the nations and the peoples.

The two witnesses are the ambassadors of the kingdom of God in the kingdom of Antichrist. John sees in a vision the Church of God undergoing hardship, appointed to suffer violent pressure from the kingdom of darkness. The holy city is trampled by the Gentiles for a period of 42 months. The Church finds itself on the threshing-floor where the sheaves of wheat are trampled; it is there that the Lord will thoroughly clear the floor, separating the wheat from the chaff.

At the same time that the Church is being trampled by the kingdom of darkness, it is arranged by the kingdom of God that it shall be accurately measured. A measuring reed is given to John, and the command comes to him: *'Go and measure the temple of God and the altar, and count the worshippers there'* (Revelation 11:1–2). See also Zechariah 2; Ezekiel 40:3; Revelation 21:15–16. The Lord will thoroughly try everything that is found in the life and work of the Church, to see what is properly measured in accordance with his word, and can be carried forward into the next age; but also what is of wood, hay and straw, which the Lord has to destroy.

The Church, undergoing this time of hardship, will become like the goldsmith's crucible, where the dross is separated from the gold. In the midst of this cleansing process, the holy city takes shape, the city on the hill, the prophetic community, attractive in its glory. The holy city, which is under pressure, will have representatives – ambassadors – in the world's anti-Christian regimes. These representatives will act with the same authority as Moses and Elijah.

The judgments over the world in the time of tribulation come through a Church that refuses to bow before the kingdom of Antichrist, but instead challenges it in the power of Jesus and showing his miracles.

The Exodus from Egypt and the liberation in the End Time

The message of Revelation is easier to understand if we compare the freeing of the people of Israel from Egypt with the liberation of God's people in the End Time.

Egypt	**The End Time**
Exodus	*Revelation*
The cry of the oppressed reaches up to God (Exodus 3:7–10).	The prayers of the saints reach up to God (Revelation 8:1–5).
Moses and Aaron as God's ambassadors before Pharaoh (Exodus 7:15).	The two witnesses as ambassadors of the kingdom of God before Antichrist (Revelation 11:3–8).
God's judgments over Egypt (Exodus 7–12):	God's judgments in the End Time:
1. Water changed to blood.	Revelation 8:8; 16:3.
2. Frogs.	Revelation 16:13–14.
3. Gnats.	
4. Swarms of flies.	
5. Plague on livestock.	
6. Boils and plague.	Revelation 16:2; 6:8.
7. Hail.	Revelation 16:21.
8. Locusts.	Revelation 9:1–11.
9. Darkness.	Revelation 6:12; 8:12.
10. The angel of death.	Revelation 6:8.
The Exodus – the freeing of God's people (Exodus 13:14).	*'Your redemption is drawing near'* (Luke 21:28).
The song of praise when they saw Pharaoh's army drowned in the Red Sea (Exodus 15).	Those who have been victorious over the beast sing the song of Moses and of the Lamb (Revelation 15:2–4).

The judgments over the earth in the End Time are to a great extent the same as the judgments visited on Pharaoh and Egypt. The judgments on Egypt were God's; he acted through the representatives of his people before Pharaoh. Moses and Aaron gave the ultimatum to the Antichrist of the time – the enemy of God's people.

The judgments in the End Time result from God's people having representatives who set squarely before governments and nations the choice between Christ and Antichrist. God's people will come to demand their freedom from the system of Antichrist, and the Lord will emphasise their right to freedom by punishing those governments and nations that will not give God's people freedom. This freedom will be demanded for the people of God during a time when in fact no one can buy or sell unless he bears the mark of the beast. God's people will insist on being able to live in freedom outside Antichrist's system.

When we see how God's people will act in the last times, we notice how wrongly we have acted as his people in the past; we in Sweden can see how we stood feebly by and watched our country being de-Christianised. So much of this process has happened either with the cooperation of Christians or with the Christians remaining silent. Only a few dissenting voices have been raised, and generally the Church has adjusted itself to the character of the age. Our churches have been closely linked with the state through receiving government support and contributions, and have not been a living protest movement against the process of de-Christianising and the anti-Christian powers in the state. These things can only be explained by the fact that the church in our country is still a mixture – in it are found both the living Bride of Christ, and also the dead church of Antichrist. The Church has had the allies of Antichrist within its own ranks. The spirit of lawlessness is, among other things, the spirit among Christians that leads them to call in question the word of God.

The Church in the End Time will be quite different. It will come to consist of a prophetic minority, who have not adapted themselves to any ideologies or community systems, but live their own lives in accordance with God's word as a called-out body of people. In this way the Church will come to stand out as a completely separate alternative, giving to mankind new possibilities and a new hope.

Confrontation with the demonic powers of Egypt

When Moses served the Lord in a ministry of liberation for God's people in captivity, he challenged the gods of Egypt through the judgments of the Lord over the land. God pronounced judgment on Egypt's gods through Moses' acts of power (Exodus 12:12; Numbers 33:4).

Pharaoh was looked on by the Egyptians as a god-king. They considered that a pharaoh became God through his birth being a divine act. When Moses went to Pharaoh and challenged him in God's name, it was the Lord, through Moses, challenging a false god.

In Egypt too, a **snake-goddess** was worshipped. Moses challenged this snake-goddess with an act of power, when Aaron's staff became a snake and swallowed up the staffs of the Egyptian sorcerers that had become snakes also.

The **river Nile** was holy in the same sense that the river Ganges is holy in India. When Moses changed its waters into blood, he was challenging something that the Egyptians regarded as holy.

The Egyptians worshipped the **sun-god** under a number of different names, such as Re, Amon-Re and (later) Aten. When darkness fell over Egypt for three days, God was showing that he was Lord over the sun-god of the Egyptians and that their sun-worship was in vain.

Frogs in Egypt were holy animals, which were not allowed to be killed, in the same way that monkeys in India are regarded as holy by the Hindus. Through Moses' act of power the houses in Egypt were filled with frogs, which the people had no right to kill.

Moses went on challenging the false gods of Egypt continuously through all his acts of power. Behind these gods stood demonic powers, even Satan himself, who seeks to be worshipped by men in various guises. John Davis in his book

Moses and the gods of Egypt has gone into the Egyptian mythology in great detail and has shown how Moses' acts of power were all the time challenging the whole system of false gods existing in Egypt.

The final judgment struck every family, when the angel of death went through the land and struck the first-born of each family that did not have the protection of the blood over the door-frame. Pharaoh had earlier given orders that all male children of the people of Israel were to be killed. This corresponds to abortion in our time, which prevents the growth of a people. One day, God's judgment came on Egypt on the grounds of the killing of children.

Because the judgments in the book of Revelation resemble the judgments on Egypt to such an extent, we may assume that behind the scenes in the End Time the same confrontation will be going on between the people of God and the false gods, the demonic powers. This helps us to understand the task fulfilled by the two witnesses in the End Time.

The two witnesses were a torment to the inhabitants of the earth

When the two witnesses have been killed by the beast, the inhabitants of the earth gloat over them and celebrate by sending each other gifts, because these two prophets had tormented them (Revelation 11:10). This shows how well they had done their work as the representatives of God's kingdom.

Elijah was a torment to Ahab. *'Is that you, you troubler of Israel?'* said Ahab when he saw Elijah. It was when Elijah had challenged Ahab's action in introducing the worship of false gods into Israel. When Ahab went on into economic crime and the murder of Naboth for the sake of his vineyard, Elijah stood in his way when he went to take possession of the vineyard. *'So you have found me, my enemy!'* said Ahab to Elijah (1 Kings 21).

John the Baptist was a torment to Herod and Herodias, because he accused them of their immoral life-style.

In the same way, the Church will be a torment to the authorities who bring in anti-Christian laws, as for example homosexual marriage. We shall be a torment to those who favour a law that allows abortion on demand, to an authority that forbids a doctor to pray with his patients, and to authorities that will not act within their powers to put an end to prostitution and sex-clubs, or to violent pornography on video, and so on.

The Church has been too soft-skinned up to now. It needs to put on a coat of thick camel-hair, as befits the ministry of Elijah.

The last days will be full of birth-pains (Matthew 24:8). Why birth-pains? It is the child to be born that causes the birth-pains, and we bear the kingdom of God within us. God's people in the End Time will be like a pregnant woman crying out in pain as she is about to give birth (Revelation 12:2). When we give out the kingdom of God, we cause repulsion in the kingdom of darkness; we cause torment, and this torment is a part of the work of giving birth to new things. We should never be afraid of causing torment to the system of Antichrist.

Martyrs after the task is completed

The protection given to the two witnesses accords with the task given to them. They are protected in order to complete their task, but after that, they are put to death by the beast (Revelation 11:7–13).

It is said of the beast that he was given power to make war against the saints and to conquer them (Revelation 13:7); but his power relates only to their bodies. Later, John sees those who had been victorious over the beast (Revelation 15:2). The martyrs are to reach a definite number (Revelation 6:9–11). Antichrist will kill many of them (Revelation 13:15; 13:7); but the martyrs will hold a place of honour in Christ's kingdom of peace (Revelation 20:4).

The Church will grow up into the fullness of Christ. Christ gave his life, and among the gifts in the Body of Christ there is the gift of the grace of martyrdom. Peter Wagner believes that Paul in 1 Corinthians 13 enumerates different gifts in the Body of Christ when he says *'If I give all I possess to the poor and surrender my body to the flames, but have not love ...'* (13:3).

171

In his book *Your Spiritual Gifts can Help your Church Grow*, Peter Wagner defines martyrdom as follows: 'The gift of martyrdom is a special ability that God has given to certain members of the Body of Christ to undergo suffering for the faith even to death while consistently displaying a joyous and victorious attitude that brings glory to God.' In order that the Body of Christ can reach its fullness in proper relation to the fullness that is found in Christ, there must be certain proportions between evangelists, pastors, apostles and martyrs, and so on.

The great prostitute was drunk with the blood of the martyrs (Revelation 17:6). Judgment came upon Babylon, Antichrist's headquarters, because in her was found the blood of the prophets and of the saints (Revelation 18:24). The Lord will demand retribution for the apostles and prophets who are killed by Antichrist's system.

There were two churches in Asia Minor that were commended by the risen Lord Jesus: Smyrna and Philadelphia. Smyrna was the suffering church (Revelation 2:10); but Philadelphia was promised that it would be a protected church (Revelation 3:10).

When the people of Israel were in Egypt and the judgments of God were falling upon the land, the Lord gave them special protection; when the Egyptian cattle died, not even one of the animals of the Israelites died (Exodus 9:7). When darkness came over Egypt for three days, all the Israelites had light in the places where they lived (Exodus 10:23). In the same way, the Lord will also protect his Church in time of hardship. So we shall see both the suffering church, Smyrna, and the protected church, Philadelphia: Christ can be glorified through life or through death. It is good to glorify Christ through one's death (John 21:18–19).

The Lord has taken his great power

Immediately after John's description of the two witnesses, he tells us of the triumph prevailing in the heavenly world.

'There were loud voices in heaven, which said: "The kingdom of this world has become the kingdom of our Lord

172

> *and of his Christ, and he will reign for ever and ever." And the twenty-four elders, who were seated on their thrones before God, fell on their faces and worshipped God, saying: "We give thanks to you, Lord God Almighty, the One who is and who was, because you have taken your great power and have begun to reign"'*   (Revelation 11:15–17)

Heaven is beginning to raise the shout of triumph in advance. So far, the Lord has not yet appeared visibly on the earth; but nevertheless heaven believes that the reign of Messiah has already begun, that he has taken his great power and begun to reign. Heaven rejoices that the two witnesses, as advance representatives of the people of God, represent the power of the Lord, and that in this sense the Lord's government of the earth has at last begun.

When God's people enter into their responsibility for interceding for their nation; when we stand so close to the 'Lord of the whole earth' that we can hear his instructions; when we receive prophetic information and can act upon it; and when we challenge Satan in every advance he tries to make, then heaven believes that the Lord's reign has begun. It does not begin at the same time as the Lord's kingdom of peace, when Jesus comes to the Mount of Olives. The Lord's reign among his people begins in hardship. In the darkest times of all, the Church will be at its most triumphant, at its position of greatest power with God.

Chapter 15

The Army of the Lamb

In the war against the great prostitute and the kingdom of Antichrist, the army of the Lamb will be mobilised and sent into battle at the decisive moment. *'They* [the ten kings] *will make war against the Lamb, but the Lamb will overcome them because he is Lord of lords and King of kings – and with him will be his called, chosen and faithful followers'* (Revelation 17:14).

In Revelation 14, we find a crowd of people who follow the Lamb wherever he goes. The Church should have no difficulty in identifying itself with this crowd who follow the Lamb, but the evil one has laid a smokescreen over this message, through the Jehovah's Witnesses' appropriation of the text concerning the 144,000. Preachers of the Word are ashamed of preaching on something that has been so severely compromised. Now is the time to take back this message from the delusion that has been put upon it. Satan's distortions are intended to frighten us and stop us from seeing what is important in God's plan.

Certainly we are the crowd who follow the Lamb. The bride is called the wife of the Lamb (Revelation 21:9); and the wedding is the wedding of the Lamb (Revelation 19:7). The apostles are called the Lamb's twelve apostles (Revelation 21:14). The 144,000 in Revelation 14 are those who follow the Lamb. The Church is the Lamb's Church and army, because he has purchased them with his precious blood. The Lamb's army will be thrown into battle against the kingdom of Antichrist; it is a fighting unit of the restored Church.

The first recruit to the Lamb's army

The Apostle John was the first one to follow the Lamb where he was going. 'Following the Lamb wherever he goes' is a good description of how John became a disciple of Jesus (John 1:35–39). John had earlier been a faithful disciple of John the Baptist, but when John the Baptist pointed to the Lamb, John immediately grasped the prophetic sign and was ready to make the break. He began to follow the Lamb wherever he went, not knowing where they were heading for. John the Baptist was the one who took the initiative in mobilising the first recruits for the army of the Lamb. In the same way the Elijah ministry will mobilise the army of the Lamb in the End Time.

The Church that reaches maturity in the fullness of Christ

One way of describing fullness and maturity is by using numbers, saying 12 times 12 times 1,000 equals 144,000. The Church, through this maturing process, will attain full manhood and the fullness of Christ (Ephesians 4:13). The Gentiles will attain their fullness (Romans 11:25). Saying that the Lamb's army will consist of 144,000 it is a way of saying that it has attained its fullness in every sense, in numbers, in maturity, in making use of gifts of grace, in spiritual authority, in prayer war, and in fully-grown development of prophecy. This maturing process has gone on through the centuries by means of restoration, which reaches its peak when the Church is ready and prepared for the kingdom tasks needed for the shift into the next age.

The group standing with the Lamb on Mount Zion

> *'Then I looked, and there before me was the Lamb, standing on Mount Zion, and with him 144,000 who had his name and his Father's name written on their foreheads.'*
> (Revelation 14:1)

The most usual way of interpreting this is that we see in this passage a group who have reached heaven and are no longer to be found on earth. But instead of this, let us harmonise the word with Hebrews 12:22:

'But you have come to Mount Zion, to the heavenly Jerusalem, the city of the living God. You have come to thousands upon thousands of angels in joyful assembly.'

We here on earth are already seated in the heavenly realms with Christ (Ephesians 2:6). We sit with Christ on his throne, and when all things are put under his feet, we share in his position of power. By the revelation of the Spirit, we understand how great a gift has been given to God's children. This revelation is like a sudden spiritual jerk that lifts us up to the throne. The woman crying out in the pain of childbirth (Revelation 12:1–5) saw her child snatched up to the throne, the child who was to rule with an iron sceptre. To stand on Mount Zion implies that we have received spiritual authority from Christ. It is that part of the Church that has understood its position of power, that will actually reign with Christ. The army of the Lamb has been equipped with the Lamb's authority.

The Father's name written on their foreheads

At the end of the age, the time for compromise is over, the separation has taken place, and people are marked to show to whom they belong. Some have the mark of the beast on their foreheads (Revelation 13:16); but others have the Father's name written on their foreheads (Revelation 14:1). Some have sold themselves to the system of Antichrist, and others have put themselves in the Father's care because of their great need. A father recognises his children and takes care of them. Before the powers of destruction are released over the world in the time of wrath, the Lord will mark his servants with his seal on their foreheads (Revelation 7:1–4). Before the judgment fell on Jerusalem, an angel was called to put a mark on the foreheads of all those who were grieving and lamenting over all the detestable things being done in her (Ezekiel 9:1–4). The army of the Lamb are given special protection under God's care during the persecution by Antichrist.

Joseph – a prototype of the 144,000

When I studied the 144,000, I asked myself whether there was any personality in the Bible who corresponded in every way with the description given to us of these people of God. If I could find such a person, it would give me the key to the understanding of the army of the Lamb. He would be the ideal prophetic prototype.

Joseph had not defiled himself with women. His purity was tested in Potiphar's house through Potiphar's wife continually trying to tempt him: 'Come to bed with me!' Not defiling oneself with women has nothing to do with marriage. Later on, Joseph married and had children. His cleanness consisted in his not yielding to sexual licence and lawlessness.

Joseph was also tested to see whether there was truth or falsehood in his speech. The test came when he was called upon to interpret the dream which the chief baker had in prison. Even though the interpretation of the dream was that the man would be put to death within three days, Joseph dared to give him the message without using any lie or half-truth to make it more acceptable. Not having any lie in one's mouth means not distorting God's prophetic message, neither adding to it nor taking away from it, not blunting or adapting the prophetic to suit the system of Antichrist which is built on compromise, adjustment, lies and propaganda.

Redeemed from the earth and from mankind

In order that this crowd could follow the Lamb wherever he went, it was necessary that they should live in freedom, that they should have been redeemed from the earth and redeemed from mankind (Revelation 14:3–4 RSV).

Joseph was sold by his brothers as a slave to Egypt, but when it was the right moment for the visions of his youth to be fulfilled, he was released from prison. Instead of being locked in Pharaoh's prison, he was given the keys of all the store-houses of Egypt. We have been under the power of Satan and of darkness, just as the whole world lies under the control of the evil one. We had a powerful gaoler over us – Satan. Satan has ruled on earth for so long that he has completely infiltrated the workings of the community and of the world, so that all mankind are captives to a greater or lesser extent. But Jesus has bought our freedom with his own blood, so that we are no longer our own, but belong to him and to his kingdom. The redeemed multitude were also marked with the name of the Lamb – a mark of ownership.

When the army of the Lamb, freed in this way, comes forward, we shall remember that many people are captives of agreements and covenants with Satan. It is said of Antichrist, *'He will confirm a covenant with many'* (Daniel 9:27). According to one Bible commentator, this means that he takes an existing covenant and makes it even more binding.

Isaiah prophesies about a time when people will make a covenant with death, an agreement with the grave (Isaiah 28:15). There are today, in the occult world, many kinds of covenants with secret initiation ceremonies that feature symbols of death, such as putting a person in a coffin. The skull and crossbones may be used, or the initiate may have to drink from a chalice mixed with blood, and to make promises under oath.

Even among Christians there are some who have entered into secret covenants as Freemasons, Oddfellows, Knights Templars, or Crusader Knights. All those things leave people with divided loyalties. Many have lost their freedom in following the Lamb by being bound up in other loyalties; winning one's freedom lies in coming out of all such ties. If this costs us our position in the community, our freedom in Christ is of far greater worth.

To be redeemed from the earth and from mankind will be a unique position, because most people will be bound by the system of Antichrist and tied to one another in large collectives or corporations, where the individual is paralysed, deprived of all initiative. But there will be a group of people who have not compromised, but have used their freedom in the service of the Lamb's own initiative.

The song of the Lamb

The army of the Lamb have learnt to sing the song of the Lamb. John came to know by revelation from Jesus that the song of praise, and singing in the Spirit, would break out among God's people in the End Time.

> *'And they sang a new song before the throne and before the four living creatures and the elders. No one could learn the song except the 144,000 who had been redeemed from the earth.'*
> (Revelation 14:3–4)

Through the song of praise, we are caught up and brought near to the throne.

Just as John the Baptist was able to initiate Jesus into his Messianic ministry through baptism, so will the prophetic Church anoint Messiah as king over the earth through the song of praise. The army of the Lamb will use the praise-song as a weapon to bind and discourage the enemy in the spirit world. When the Lord executes his judgments in the time of wrath, those judgments will be accompanied by the song of praise from those who know that the Lord is also righteous and just when he executes his judgments of wrath on the earth. Through singing in the Spirit, we know that God's people today can be caught up to the throne, where they hear, in the Spirit, the song of praise of the angels before the throne, and learn to express with their tongues what they hear in their spirit.

The first-fruits

'They were purchased from among men and offered as first-fruits to God and the Lamb' (Revelation 14:4). In an army there are elite troops, such as paratroops, Commandos, or the Gurkhas from Nepal. They are elite soldiers, chosen for the most difficult tasks. In the army of the Lord there is also a force of first-fruits, but it is not a question of A-class and B-class Christians. The first-fruits of a harvest were a sacrifice consecrated to the Lord so that all the remainder of the harvest would become holy. The Lord wants to have a first-fruits force in each nation, who will go out in front so that all God's people can be sanctified. Some must be separated from the main body and go out in front so that all may be saved.

Certainly the renewal concerns all God's people, but we cannot for ever stand waiting for those who do not want to go on further. Caring for the Body, simply the belief that the renewal concerns all the people of God, means that we must go on further. A situation soon arises where it is clear that we are sent to save many.

Joseph was more loved by his father than his brothers were, but that implied that he was chosen to save his father and his brothers during a severe famine. Despite all misunderstanding, envy and treachery, Joseph was able to meet his brothers with no feeling of bitterness, because he had understood his calling as the first of the flock.

> *'I am your brother Joseph, the one you sold into Egypt! And now, do not be distressed and do not be angry with yourselves for selling me here, because ... God sent me ahead of you to preserve for you a remnant on earth and to save your lives by a great deliverance.'*   (Genesis 45:4–7)

It is difficult to be an elite soldier of the Lord in today's Western culture of organisation, which in many places insists that all men are created equal, to such an extent that no one is allowed to rise above his fellows. Only in sport and in pop music is it permissible to become a star, but otherwise in general we are condemned to remain a grey mass, flattened down and docile, with no one allowed to deviate from the norm or to create disorder in the ranks; nor is anyone free to excel in wisdom, personality, ideas or success. The Lord, however, wants to take the individual out of the mass; our freedom has been purchased for us so that we can go in front and save others. You must dare to go out in front, to be the first-fruits, to live before your time, to say yes to a calling that sometimes separates you from the mass.

A Swedish Christian journalist, Bo Pax Göransson, has written about the effects of collective thinking in these terms: 'The collective has no conscience; it is only private individuals who have consciences. When people are bound together in great collectives, there can be no Christian, conscience-controlled politics in our country. What does a person do with his conscience when it is only given the choice between two great collectives, both full of lies? It is the personal considerations of conscience, unfettered by the lies of the collective, that are the foundations of justice. One party leader has said: A government has a collective responsibility for what it does and what it says. Its individual members cannot go out and fly the flag with personal opinions on different questions. This is the formal democratic society, built on a collective that has no conscience. Collectives that are not renewed by the consciences of individuals eventually lead to the collapse of the law-governed society. The collective, restricted by the law like the earlier kings of Sweden, has no right to compel or cause to compel anyone's conscience, as it was written in the law of old.'

A lamb without blemish

Jesus was a lamb without spot or blemish, and the Lamb's people must follow the Lamb in conduct without blemish. *'These are those who did not defile themselves with women, for they kept themselves pure ... No lie was found in their mouths; they are blameless'* (Revelation 14:4–5).

There are no perfect men or women, but there are personalities that have stood the test. Joseph was tested in both these areas, in Potiphar's house and in the prison. He did not succumb to the attempted seduction by Potiphar's wife, and no lie was found in his prophetic message.

The signs by which we shall recognise the kingdom of Antichrist are sexual uncleanness and lies. Antichrist comes with a big mouthful of propaganda full of all the acts of power generated by lies. The great prostitute will seduce the kings of the earth and all its inhabitants (Revelation 17:2); we have seen the wave of pornography, and can understand that this is not mere picture-language. The spearhead of lawlessness is moral decline. Anyone who has broken God's law through unfaithfulness or adultery soon takes a further step into economic crime or unfaithfulness to his country.

The army of the Lamb must be clean in those areas where the world has failed.

Redeemed to follow the Lamb

The army of the Lamb is made up of people of God who have been freed by reconciliation with God through Jesus, set free from all that binds people to the community and all wrong loyalties to men, free in their consciences to follow the voice of conscience. In this way, they can remain entirely at the disposal of the Lamb.

Paul was careful to maintain this freedom. *'Am I not free? Am I not an apostle?'* (1 Corinthians 9:1). The apostles and the prophets should all be free.

The Lord needs people for the army of the Lamb who have been set free for different tasks that cannot be made to conform with normal job descriptions in any church or Christian organisation. Church members can be so occupied with perfectly legitimate activities that they never manage to pray. Bureaucracy keeps us bound up by paperwork, something that is part of the system of Antichrist. The army of the Lamb are those who are set free, so that they never need to make the excuse 'I haven't time', when the Lord wants something done. On days of prayer and fasting, it sometimes happens that the church members rush about and make excuses for themselves that they do not have time to pray, while other Christians, who belong to other church traditions, turn up and seem to have plenty of time. Even today earthly goods, the home, marriage, and the cares of this world, hinder people so that they are not set free to accept the invitations of the kingdom of heaven.

In God's kingdom, people are needed who have gone out in faith into a freedom that waits to be sent wherever the Lamb may command. Therefore, put your affairs into order in such a way that you can be free for some years to carry out exceptional tasks, such as: working to get the Jews out of the former Soviet Union; exposing the economy of Antichrist when it sneaks into your country's economy; and following and dealing with the encroachments of lawlessness into your country's legislation, keeping a careful watch on what is going on in the area of family law in particular. There are numerous tasks to be done in the kingdom that neither churches nor other organisations can fit into their conditions of office, and there will be a need for many thousands of men and women of God for just such tasks during the transition period into the next age.

Are you free, so far as time and place are concerned, to be

sent anywhere at short notice? Are you free to spend a month quietly seeking the Lord in prayer and fasting?

I believe that the Church should take the initiative in giving this kind of freedom. I myself am serving in a local church with full freedom to do whatever the Lord may say, and to go wherever he may want me to go, anywhere in the world.

The marks of the Lamb's army

The army that the Lamb will assemble to make war against the ten kings in the revived Roman Empire are the called, chosen and faithful ones (Revelation 17:14). To understand this, we can look further at Joseph's life:

Joseph was called. While he was still young, he received two prophetic dreams, in which his calling was revealed to him and his task described. His brothers and his parents would come and bow before him. These dreams were fulfilled.

Joseph was chosen. He was chosen through his father's love. Israel loved Joseph more than any of his other sons, because he had been born to him in his old age (Genesis 37:3). We are chosen through God's love; his love has called us out of the world in order to stand on his behalf.

Joseph was faithful. His faith was tested for many years, through the envy of his brothers and their treachery when they sold him into Egypt. His faith was further tested in Potiphar's house, and in the prison, right up to the day when the Lord knew that he had a reliable servant who could be put in charge of much, even in charge of all the storehouses of Egypt. It needs obedience, hard testing, and much time, to train faithful servants in the Lord's army.

Joseph was reliable in carrying out the task his father gave him in sending him to his brothers when they were grazing their father's flocks: *'Go and see if all is well with your brothers'*: (Genesis 37:14). In fact, he never completed this task. But when the famine came and his brothers stood in front of him, he fulfilled what his father had asked him to do, in meeting his brothers' needs. He was faithful to the vision of his calling.

The Lamb and his faithful ones will conquer the ten kings

The battle in Revelation 17 concerns ten kings in a resurgent Roman Empire. These kings receive authority for a short time as kings along with the beast. Daniel sees how the Roman Empire is of mixed iron and clay (Daniel 2). This means that the ten kings are very vulnerable if one can hit the cracks in the clay, and they are in fact defeated by the army of the Lamb.

The fighting starts when the ten kings make war against the Lamb: we therefore watch carefully to see what persons or organisations turn against Jesus Christ in speech, writing or actions. When they have begun the battle, then it becomes our turn to intervene. When Goliath blasphemed the God of Israel, the battle had begun for David, and he knew that he had the Lord on his side in that battle.

The battle is fought out as we, like Moses and Elijah, or like the two witnesses, make use of the gifts of working miracles, the prophetic gifts, prayer war, the prayer of authority, fasting, and the song of praise. The army of the Lamb sing a new song, the song of Moses and of the Lamb. They sing the song of victory, even before Babylon and Antichrist are defeated.

The Lamb's army will pray for judgments to fall on Babylon (Revelation 18:6–7). Isaiah saw how the battle would be fought against those who have entered into a covenant with death and with the grave, and have hidden themselves by taking refuge in a lie (Isaiah 28:14–21). Day after day the scourge will sweep over them like an overwhelming flood. *'The Lord will rise up as he did at Mount Perazim, he will rouse himself as in the Valley of Gibeon.'*

What happened at Mount Perazim? It was at Baal Perazim that the Lord twice gave David victory over the Philistines (2 Samuel 5:17–25). In both battles David and his army had to follow the Lord's instructions precisely, a picture of following the Lamb wherever he goes. *'As soon as you hear the sound of marching in the tops of the balsam trees, move quickly, because that will mean the Lord has gone out in front of you to strike the Philistine army.'* The army of the Lamb must first follow in the Lamb's footsteps.

And what happened at Gibeon? It was there that Joshua defeated the Amorites. In that valley, Joshua commanded the sun to stand still, and the Lord hurled large hailstones down on the Amorites from the sky (Joshua 10:7–13). This will be repeated when the kingdom of Antichrist is destroyed. *'From the sky huge hailstones of about a hundred pounds each fell upon men. And they cursed God on account of the plague of hail, because the plague was so terrible'* (Revelation 16:21). The Lord does not only make war with the help of the powers of nature in this battle; it is fought together with the army of the Lamb.

Recently a preacher asked: 'Have you ever been in a prayer gathering where those who were praying asked that all the events of the Book of Revelation would be fulfilled?' We answered no, but during that day of prayer we did pray through the various happenings spoken of in Revelation. The kingdom of Antichrist will be defeated by those who understand God's purposes in accordance with Revelation, and are able in every way to work together with the Lord in carrying them out, so that his kingdom will be restored on earth and all rebellion will be crushed.

Chapter 16

The Friend of the Bridegroom

John the Baptist had a special relationship with the bridegroom, Jesus Christ, so that he was able to be called the friend of the bridegroom. It is the task of the friend of the bridegroom to bring the bride and the bridegroom together. John said of himself:

> *'I am not the Christ but am sent ahead of him. The bride belongs to the bridegroom. The friend who attends the bridegroom waits and listens for him, and is full of joy when he hears the bridegroom's voice. That joy is mine, and it is now complete.'* (John 3:28, 29)

In many parts of Asia and Africa, it is the custom for a friend of the bridegroom to be the intermediary in arranging a marriage. He does the negotiating, makes the proposal on behalf of the bridegroom, and is involved in the preparations for the marriage. In Pakistan, where I was a missionary for eleven years, it was usual for the parents and the head of the family to arrange the wedding, but they often used to come to a pastor or a missionary and ask that someone should act as go-between to seek a suitable bride for the bridegroom. It could happen that during a pastors' conference, one of the pastors would describe some young man and ask for help, to see if there might be a suitable bride for him in one of the other churches.

The aim for the friend of the bridegroom is to produce a

bride who is full of love, who gladly says 'yes', and who is full of joyful anticipation as she awaits the coming of the bridegroom. Among his tasks is to watch over all the bride's preparations, to follow the bride all the way, and to be with her when she is presented to the bridegroom. The friend looks on with great joy in the fulfilment of his task, when the bride finds the bridegroom.

If you are willing to carry out an Elijah ministry, I would like to give you the responsibility of finding a bride who will say 'yes' to the Bridegroom Jesus. Many Christians are full of fear about the coming of Jesus. Our aim should be to create in the Bride a joyful, forward-looking attitude concerning the coming of the King. Every meeting or service in the Christian Church should be as full of anticipation and love, light and joy, as when the church building is decorated for the wedding and the church sits waiting for the moment when they will hear the music of the wedding march and see the bride and her followers enter in procession.

A wedding song for the king from the friend of the bridegroom

At a wedding it is usual to have congratulatory speeches, and often to express congratulations in song or poetry. Psalm 45 is a poem about love, written for the wedding of a king by someone who was a friend of both the bride and the bridegroom. We can identify ourselves with the writer of this psalm, and set our own emotional life and will in the context of his words.

First, the friend speaks to the bridegroom:

> *'My heart is stirred by a noble theme as I recite my verses for the king; my tongue is the pen of a skilful writer. You are the most excellent of men and your lips have been anointed with grace, since God has blessed you for ever. Gird your sword upon your side, O mighty one; clothe yourself with splendour and majesty. In your majesty ride forth victoriously on behalf of truth, humility and righteousness; let your right hand display awesome deeds. Let*

*your sharp arrows pierce the hearts of the king's enemies;
let the nations fall beneath your feet. Your throne, O God,
will last for ever and ever; a sceptre of justice will be the
sceptre of your kingdom. You love righteousness and hate
wickedness; therefore God, your God, has set you above
your companions by anointing you with the oil of joy.'*

(Psalm 45:1–7)

We accept that the song of praise in this psalm is about
Jesus, because the letter to the Hebrews quotes this psalm and
applies it to Jesus (Hebrews 1:8–9).

The characteristics of the friend of the bridegroom are his
deep love and admiration for the bridegroom. He has seen all
his good sides; he wants to draw attention to the richness of his
personality and the greatness of his power, so that everyone
will take notice of them. The friend is willing to do anything
for the bridegroom, and he can be recognised by his song of
praise to the bridegroom.

The friend of the bridegroom talks to the bride

He gives advice on the wedding day:

*'Listen, O daughter, consider and give ear: Forget your
people, and your father's house. The king is enthralled by
your beauty; honour him, for he is your lord.'*

(Psalm 45:10–11)

The friend of the bridegroom fears that the bride's thoughts
may be divided or not concentrated. He warns her to forget
her people and her father's house. There should be no home-
sickness occupying her mind, no love of this world and of the
mind of this age. The friend of the bridegroom wants to see
the bride giving herself wholly to the bridegroom, so that he
can delight in her beauty. Applying this to the Church, it
means handing ourselves over completely to Christ. He cannot
delight in her beauty if at the same time she has loyalties to the
world and the seeds of unfaithfulness in her thoughts. In his
speech, the friend warns that her attitude should be one of
submission, reverence and adoration before the bridegroom.

A word of warning about gifts from Tyre

The friend of the bridegroom continues and says to the bride:

> 'The Daughter of Tyre will come with a gift, men of wealth
> will seek your favour.'   (Psalm 45:12)

It is possible to read a warning into these words. On the wedding day, the bride naturally receives many presents; but presents can also be given with false motives, when someone with selfish interests seeks to gain advantages from knowing the bride. It is particularly dangerous when the gifts come from Tyre. Tyre stands in Ezekiel 27–28 for the spirit of trade, which came into Lucifer and caused him to fall. Tyre stands also for the business covenant that Solomon made with the king of Tyre, Hiram, which indirectly caused his fall. It stands too for the spirit of Babylon in the last times. Tyre stands in the word of God for a world economy that has no room for God's plans. Tyre has taken the silver and the gold, which were the Lord's, and has carried off his treasures (Joel 3:5).

The bride has to be warned about something that could become a snare for her and draw her interest away from the bridegroom; but these words can also mean that the riches of Mammon can be turned to a good use as wedding gifts for the bride.

Isaiah prophesied about Tyre hiring herself as a prostitute, saying that these unrighteously acquired resources would ultimately be consecrated to the Lord.

> 'At the end of seventy years, the Lord will deal with Tyre.
> She will return to her hire as a prostitute and will ply her
> trade with all the kingdoms on the face of the earth. Yet her
> profit and her earnings will be set apart for the Lord; they
> will not be stored up or hoarded. Her profits will go to
> those who live before the Lord, for abundant food and fine
> clothes.'   (Isaiah 23:17–18)

The collected riches of Mammon, the silver and the gold that Satan has stolen from God, will all be given as a wedding present to the Bride of Christ, but then she herself must be sanctified and live before the face of the Lord, freed from Tyre's spirit of trade, in order for these miracles to take place. The Lord is going to free resources for the evangelisation of the world. If we interpret Isaiah's message literally, it means that the children of prostitutes and porn-kings will be saved, and will give the wealth they have inherited, even though it was acquired through unrighteousness, towards evangelism.

The friend of the bridegroom sees the bride installed in her chamber

It is only the closest relatives and friends who can see the fully-dressed bride in the room where she waits to be brought forth in accordance with Eastern custom. The bride remains hidden from public view; but the friend of the bridegroom has seen the bride, dressed and ready:

> *'All glorious is the princess within her chamber; her gown is interwoven with gold. In embroidered garments she is led to the king; her virgin companions follow her and are brought to you. They are led in with joy and gladness; they enter the palace of the king.'* (Psalm 45:13–15)

Those who carry out an Elijah ministry in the last days will take part in preparing the bride, and will see her, when she stands fully prepared and wearing her bridal clothes. It is through prophetic ministry that the bride will be made ready. The message of the prophet is itself the water of cleansing in which the bride will bathe herself in order to be clean.

> *'Christ loved the church and gave himself up for her to make her holy, cleansing her by the washing with water through the word.'* (Ephesians 5:25–26)

'The word' here means the *rhema*, the prophetic word. When Jesus wanted to cleanse the seven churches of Asia Minor, he gave them a cleansing bath by sending a prophetic word to each of the churches. This prophetic word was like a mirror, showing where the stains and wrinkles were. It is in the power of the cleansing waters that the church will be set forth in glory for the wedding, without stain or wrinkle or any other blemish. The Elijah ministry plays a most important part in the preparation of the bride for her wedding.

Chapter 17

Bringing the King back to the Earth

During a worship service, someone gave this prophetic message from the Lord: 'I, the Lord, have chosen you to do the deeds that will bring Christ back as king over the whole earth.' When I received this prophetic message, my inmost being was filled with zeal and enthusiasm. I wondered, however, and I sought the answer from the Lord. What are the things I should be doing in order to hasten his coming? In the following pages I will tell you what some of these things are. As the time is getting near, the Lord is going to show us, through revelation in the prophetic word, how we can act prophetically.

We can share in hastening the coming of Jesus: '... *as you look forward to the day of God and speed its coming'* (2 Peter 3:12).

When Jesus came the first time, a long series of people had all contributed to preparing for his coming. Some of these people were his own ancestors. When Ruth made her declaration of loyalty to Naomi, it was an act that brought her into the genealogy of Jesus. When Samuel anointed David as king, he prepared the family line from which Jesus would be born.

When Jesus taught his disciples to pray 'Our Father', he showed that we are involved in the process of making God's kingdom come on earth. We are not mere spectators of this process, but we are to pray continually for it.

When Jesus lived on this earth, he was constantly fulfilling prophecies. Sometimes it happened unconsciously, but we can be sure that Jesus knew the Scriptures and purposely fulfilled prophecies. When he said or did anything, Matthew, for example, could say: *'Then what was said through the prophet Jeremiah was fulfilled'* (Matthew 2:17). Jesus worked in harmony with the prophetic word.

The Church finds itself, in the same way, in the centre of the action, as if inside a prophetic workshop, where from time to time we step into the prophetic scene by consciously doing acts on which we have been given light by the word of God.

Do we want him to come?

When we speak about bringing Christ back to the earth, and doing those things that hasten his coming, we must be quite clear in our minds where the accent lies when we talk about the coming of Jesus. It is not the Rapture of the Church that is the most important event surrounding his coming. Even though Enoch was the subject of a rapture, he prophesied: *'See, the Lord is coming with thousands upon thousands of his holy ones'* (Jude 14). He put the emphasis on the coming of Jesus to earth. Even Daniel emphasised the coming of Messiah.

> *'There before me was one like a son of man, coming with the clouds of heaven ... He was given authority, glory and sovereign power; all peoples, nations and men of every language worshipped him ... But the saints of the Most High will receive the kingdom and will possess it for ever.'*
> (Daniel 7:13–14, 17)

We must reclaim more strongly the emphasis of the prophets that he will actually come to earth.

There has been a line of preaching that has created fear of his coming. People have preached on the text, *'One will be taken and the other left'*, in such a way that the preaching has emphasised the terrible fate of the ones who are left behind, and this has caused people to fear the coming of Jesus.

The preaching, 'Jesus is coming; are you ready?' has caused many to take stock of their preparedness. It becomes a teaching of works, where hardly anyone is quite sure whether he has attained the required standard. 'I have won five people for Christ; is that enough so as to be ready for his coming, or must I win ten?' I was asked by someone who was anxious about the coming.

When the coming of Christ has been divided up into episodes, the Rapture has often been emphasised more than Christ's coming to earth. Those who know their responsibility for the earth have difficulty in praying for an evacuation. The coming in the clouds can become an attempt to escape from the problems of this world. The coming means that there must be an arrival, followed by a presence. Jesus is coming to be present on earth. The Rapture is only the regrouping of the Church so as to be at the centre of the action when Jesus comes to be king over the earth. Even if there is to be an interval of time between the Rapture and the return of the King with his Saints, there is still no doubt about where the emphasis lies in Scripture for the fulfilment of our hopes. If we want him to come to earth, then we shall also work together doing those things that lead to his coming.

Are you going to be the first or the last in bringing back the King?

There is a prophetic picture of bringing Jesus back as king, in the account of how Judah and Israel brought King David back after the rebellion of Absalom which had forced him to flee from Jerusalem.

The king was ready to come back, and all his enemies had been removed. What was clear was the eagerness of the people to bring him back.

> 'Throughout the tribes of Israel, the people were all arguing with each other, saying: "The king delivered us from the hand of our enemies ... So why do you say nothing about bringing the king back?" King David sent this message to Zadok and Abiathar, the priests: "Ask the elders of Judah, Why should you be the last to bring the king back to his palace?"'
> (2 Samuel 19:9–11)

It was the men of Judah who took the action needed to bring the king back to Jerusalem, when they sent a message to the king: *'Return, you and all your men'* (2 Samuel 19:14). Then the king returned and came as far as the Jordan, and the men of Judah went to meet him there. After that, a dispute arose between the men of Israel and the men of Judah. The men of Israel complained that it had been they who had first suggested bringing the king back. They grumbled about Judah to the king and said, *'Why did our brothers, the men of Judah, steal the king away and bring him and his household across the Jordan, together with all his men?'* (2 Samuel 19:41).

Will the Church, or will Israel, be the first to bring Messiah back? If the Church does not awaken in zeal for the prophetic task, then it will be taken over by prophetically minded Jews.

The prophetic Church will have the initiative in bringing Jesus back as king over the earth. Those who have a prophetic calling for the End Time should come together in prayer and fasting, and listen to the Lord in order to find out: What initiative needs to be taken? What prophetic word should be spoken? What prophetic word is being fulfilled at this moment? What message should be given to God's people to get them to deal with the enormous task of preparing for the King's triumphal procession?

Crushing the Rebellion of Antichrist

Before David's faithful followers could send word to the king that he could return, they had crushed Absalom's rebellion. The prophetic Church will stand against Antichrist's power take-over and effectively crush it. This is the task of the army of the Lamb, and to understand this task, it will help to study Absalom's rebellion against David. David is a type of Christ, and Absalom's rebellion is a picture of the rebellion of Antichrist described, for instance, in Psalm 2. It was this conspiracy that forced David to leave Jerusalem. Jesus was also forced to leave Jerusalem because of the conspiracy of the Sanhedrin with Pilate, Annas, Caiaphas and Herod.

Absalom's conspiracy against David

Absalom began his rebellion by questioning David's right to judge. When anyone was seeking a judicial decision, Absalom tried to create dissatisfaction by saying to the complainant: 'Look, your claims are valid and proper, but there is no representative of the king to hear you'. And Absalom added: *'If only I were appointed judge in the land! Then everyone who has a complaint or case could come to me and I would see that he receives justice'* (2 Samuel 15:1–6). The spirit of lawlessness questions all forms of authority, such as the word of God, the ten commandments, or a country's judicial system based on God's commandments; and seeks to replace them with an entirely new world-wide system of law that has no Christian basis.

The next phase of the rebellion was a religious falsehood and lie as a cover for the conspiracy. Absalom asked his father: *'Let me go to Hebron and fulfil a vow I made to the Lord'*; and said he would be worshipping the Lord in Hebron. He did go there and he did offer sacrifices, but it was really only a cover. The conspiracy of Antichrist will be characterised by lies and religious fraud, infiltrating itself into Christian circles in preparation for the power take-over. From Hebron, Absalom sent out secret messengers. Satan is not particularly ingenious with new methods, and he always leaves behind the same visiting-card or sign of recognition at the scene of his deeds. This sign is that of secrecy, because he operates in the darkness and in secrecy. The essence of Babylon is secrecy. Paul tells us that lawlessness comes as a secret power.

Ahitophel gave Absalom the advice that he should lie with David's concubines. Absalom accepted this advice, and did it quite openly on the roof of the royal palace in the sight of all the people, to strengthen his courage and to make himself hateful to his father (2 Samuel 16:20–23). Sexual licence was appropriate to strengthen courage and create unity in the conspiracy. The prostitute will seduce the kings and all the peoples of the earth. The conspiracy of Antichrist is marked by a deliberate, systematic destruction of moral standards in people, to make them hateful to God.

The characteristic signs of the system of Antichrist are therefore the questioning of authority, lies and religious deception, indecency, and secrecy.

How David dealt with the conspiracy

David himself fled across the Jordan into the desert, but he gave orders to some of his most reliable men to remain behind in Jerusalem, where they would stay in the wasp's nest of the conspiracy, right in Antichrist's headquarters. Hushai and the priests Zadok and Abiathar stayed behind in this way.

We must today have Christians in strategic positions in our community, which is threatened with being taken over by the powers of Antichrist. Even if Antichrist does take over, the Lord will prepare the way for certain people with a special calling to be present right in Satan's headquarters, like the faithful witness Antipas who stayed in Pergamum, where Satan's throne was, and gave his life as a martyr for Jesus (Revelation 2:12–13).

Then too, there are a large number in the Church who, like David's men, will follow the king out into the desert. They have covenanted to follow the king wherever he goes, whether in honour or in humiliation, in the headquarters or out in the desert, to life or to death.

David's prayer

David prayed about Ahitophel, one of his best advisers, who had gone over to Absalom. He prayed, '*O Lord, turn Ahitophel's counsel into foolishness*' (2 Samuel 15:31). God's word says: '*I will destroy the wisdom of the wise; the intelligence of the intelligent I will frustrate*' (1 Corinthians 1:19).

Politicians, occult magicians, national economists and experts in every field will all come and give advice in preparing the kingdom of Antichrist. We shall have occasion to pray like David: 'Turn the advice of the counsellors into foolishness; let them be laughed at for their stupidity!' The same applies to those who gather together against the Lord and against his Anointed One. They will wear themselves out with their counsel (Isaiah 47:13); meanwhile we shall pray for discouragement, confusion, and madness in the system of Antichrist.

What happened then as an answer to David's prayer about Ahitophel? Absalom's men were given contradictory advice by Hushai and by Ahitophel, and they chose to follow the advice of Hushai, although that of Ahitophel would have been far more dangerous for David. If Absalom had followed Ahitophel's advice, David would have been defeated. *'For the Lord had determined to frustrate the good advice of Ahitophel in order to bring disaster on Absalom'* (2 Samuel 17:1–14). When Ahitophel saw that his advice had not been followed, he hanged himself (17:23).

'But I am a man of prayer' (Psalm 109:4) was David's secret weapon against false talk, lying tongues and words of hate. The Church is going to use the weapon of prayer to defeat the rebellion of Antichrist.

God's people's care for one another

David and his men built up their own intelligence service, and through this, David was kept fully informed of what was happening at Absalom's headquarters. Hushai brought the information to the priests, Zadok and Abiathar. Jonathan and Ahimaaz, who were staying at En Rogel, received the information through a servant girl. The two messengers were hidden in a house at Bahurim, and Absalom's men did not find them. Meanwhile there was a caring ministry at Mahanaim, where David had fled beyond the Jordan. There were three people there who had a ministry like that of Joseph, keeping a storehouse for the people of God. These people

> *'brought bedding and bowls and articles of pottery. They also brought wheat and barley, flour and roasted grain, beans and lentils, honey and curds, sheep, and cheese from cows' milk for David and his people to eat. For they said, "The people have become hungry and tired and thirsty in the desert."'*
>
> (2 Samuel 17:15–29; see also Revelation 12:6)

When we fight against Antichrist, we shall exclude ourselves from the facilities for buying and selling in the normal community (Revelation 13:17). We shall stand outside the social security system, the hospitals, insurance, and the safety of the community. Then will come the real test of how God's people care for one another. Through this care, a parallel community will be built up, which will be an alternative to the community of lies and lawlessness. God's people have their own leadership, their own economy, their own system of communication, and their own moral order.

David's men fight against Absalom's army

David mustered the men who were with him, divided them into fighting units and appointed commanders over them: commanders of thousands and commanders of hundreds. David understood that God's army needs leadership and division of responsibility in which everyone knows his task, his gifts and his ministry.

The battle itself took place in the forest of Ephraim. The army of Israel was defeated by the servants of David, and the casualties that day were great – 20,000 men; *'and the forest claimed more lives that day than the sword'*. Absalom himself got his head caught in the branches of a large oak tree as the mule he was riding went under it; the mule went on and he was left hanging. The forest worked together with David's men in the defeat of Absalom, the man of rebellion (2 Samuel 18:6–9).

When the apostles were confronted by the anti-Christian opposition from the Sanhedrin, they prayed, and began their prayer by praising the creator: *'Sovereign Lord, you made the heaven and the earth and the sea, and everything in them'* (Acts 4:24). The sun cooperated with Joshua when he needed a longer day to accomplish his defeat of the enemy. Sometimes God uses rain, sometimes fire, storm or hail to work together with his people in putting down a rebellion. In Revelation, there are instances of this cooperation between nature and the people of God in carrying out God's judgments. When God judged those who had killed the two witnesses, there was a severe earthquake (Revelation 11:13); while an even greater earthquake will happen in conjunction with the final judgment over the throne of Antichrist (Revelation 16:17–21). There are several examples of how the kingdom of Antichrist is crushed by the Lord putting the creation and the powers of nature to work against it. While the judgments of Revelation are being carried out over the earth during the time of God's wrath, an angel warns the saints to

> *'Fear God and give him glory, because the hour of his judgment has come. Worship him who made the heavens, the earth, the sea and the springs of water.'*
>
> (Revelation 14:6–7)

The prophetic Church needs to be in harmony both with the angels and also with God's creation. When word came to David of the death of Absalom, he grieved deeply. The news of the victory meant nothing to him for the moment, because he loved his rebellious son so much. In Antichrist's rebellion there will be people taking part who were once very close to Jesus. Just as he wept over Jerusalem, when he came to the Mount of Olives, so he will weep and grieve over those who are led astray into working with Antichrist.

When the rebellion of Absalom was crushed, it only remained to welcome the king back to Jerusalem.

War or Rapture?

The Church has in general been so looking towards the Rapture before the coming of the Antichrist, that we have shirked the task of fighting against Antichrist's powers. His spirit has been at work through all the ages, but there have always been Christians who were more keen to leave the world to go and be with Christ, than to make war against the destructive powers. As the army of the Lamb, we cannot welcome Jesus back to reign until we have overcome the world and defeated Antichrist.

Ezekiel spoke to the prophets in Israel and held them responsible for not having prepared God's people for the End Time battle.

> *'You have not gone up to the breaks in the wall to repair it*
> *for the house of Israel so that it will stand firm in the battle*
> *on the day of the Lord.'*   (Ezekiel 13:5)

I do not want to have that judgment upon me. I am responsible for preparing the overcoming Church to stand firm in the
battle on the day of the Lord. If the End Time Church is to be
ready for confrontation with Antichrist, I am responsible if the
Church has not been prepared for that battle. If the Rapture is
to take place before Antichrist appears on the world scene, I
will be most relieved; but if an unprepared Church has to face
the battle against Antichrist, the prophets and the leaders will
be responsible. Therefore, I am training God's people for the
End Time battle. 'Raise up the army of the Lamb, train the
officers in my army' was a word spoken by the Lord to a group
of leaders, who all stood to attention and listened because the
Commander of the Lord's army was speaking to them. I have
met the prayer-Generals in the Lord's army and we have held
'Prepare for Battle' camps where we have trained prayer
warriors.

In the final battle against Antichrist, I am going to take part,
and so will you, if you are a member of God's Church. Jesus
will come back *with* his saints. When the King of kings arrives
back, he will be accompanied by the heavenly armies on white
horses, dressed in fine linen, white and clean (Revelation
19:11–18). I myself believe in a Rapture that comes between
now and that event. Then I will fight side by side with Jesus in
a transformed, resurrected body. But the battle that I fight
today is one and the same. It is wrong to see the final battle as
a separate one; in fact, the battle has been going on for two
thousand years.

Hastening the Coming of Jesus

1. Bringing the Church into Maturity

Christ does not come to collect an immature Bride. Each step
that contributes to leading the Church into maturity, hastens
Jesus' coming. Each step that we take towards unity with those

who have life in Christ is also a step that brings him closer to being king over the earth.

We are to form men and women of God, thoroughly equipped for every good work. These people of God are those who are ready for Jesus' coming and prepared for the final tasks that the Church is to carry out. We are to bring people into restoration as Elijah people.

We are not to hold back in the matter of spiritual gifts, while we *'eagerly wait for our Lord Jesus Christ to be revealed'* (1 Corinthians 1:7). Those who serve with spiritual gifts serve their brothers and sisters; servanthood is one of the signs of a mature Church.

The Church that reaches maturity will be a releasing factor in the salvation of Israel

Paul says: *'Israel has experienced a hardening in part until the full number of the Gentiles has come in'* (Romans 11:25). What is the fullness or full number, the *pleroma* of the Gentiles? It is fullness in maturity. That maturity will be the releasing factor for the salvation of Israel.

The Church will cause Israel to envy, as Israel will recognise in the Church something that they themselves have lost. They will be able to recognise God's glory in the Church – the glory that they have lost. They will be able to recognise the pure, liberating song of praise in the Church. They will be able to see the spiritual gifts of Elijah and Elisha at work in the Church, even though they have only read the Old Testament. For they have read that Moses and Aaron had the gift of doing acts of power; that Elijah and Elisha had gifts of acts of power and of healing; and so on. What they have read in the Old Testament, they will meet as a reality in the prophetic Church in the End Time. They themselves are a divided people, but they will recognise the glory that brings unity among people, as they see the unity of the Church.

We have not yet reached such a state; there is not much in today's Church that causes envy. But we shall bring the Church into such a maturity that she is ready for her last task on earth; so that she is ready to wait for Jesus as a mature Bride.

2. Fulfilling the Great Commission

A person whose destiny in life is to bring King Jesus back to the earth must in some way or other be involved with reaching the unreached.

Jesus has given us a task to fulfil before he returns.

> *'This gospel of the kingdom will be preached in the whole world as a testimony to all nations, and then the end will come.'* (Matthew 24:14)

Here there is a very clear order of events: first the preaching, and then *'the end will come'*. Jesus will not return until all nations, tribes and ethnic groups have heard the Gospel.

The full number of the people of God is a multitude from every nation, tribe, people and language (Revelation 7:9). The Church that is going to reign with Christ will have a full representation from all nations and groups of people.

How many tribes are there? About 5,000. How many languages are there on the earth? Wycliffe Bible Translators reckon there are 5,687 different languages. How many nations or ethnic groups are there? There are more than 200 nations and thousands of ethnic groups. The remaining task is to reach about 12,000 unreached groups.

Why have they not been reached with the Gospel?

Some of them live in extreme climatic conditions far beyond the reach of modern communications. Unreached tribal people in Siberia live in areas where the winter temperature is minus 50 degrees Celsius. To reach them it is necessary to know how to drive a snow-scooter; in former times dog-sledges were used. Others live in deserts where there are no tarred roads and the heat is extreme as the sand swirls over the desert tracks. Some unreached peoples live in mountain ranges at altitudes of four or five thousand metres. There are unreached Indian tribes in the Amazon rain-forest and river areas. It can take up to forty days to get to them, by boat, canoe and on foot. The rain-forest is so dense that no helicopter can land. Earlier mission workers have left the most difficult geographical areas for later workers to overcome; so there is a need for intrepid, tough mission workers who can withstand hardships, to enable us to fulfil the missionary task and welcome Jesus back.

Other unreached groups live in places where there is great unrest, where enmity exists between groups of people causing violence or long-standing civil war between tribes or nations. Anyone seeking to reach men and women with the Gospel in areas of unrest must be willing to risk his life.

Many groups of people are unreached because they are controlled by religions or ideologies that have created hard ground for the Gospel. The majority of the unreached live in Muslim, Buddhist or Hindu countries or places where the darkness still prevails through voodoo, witchcraft or various kinds of secret brotherhoods, or in countries whose leaders have made themselves into gods. There are always spiritual reasons for an area being still closed to the Gospel, and we today can take steps against these spiritual circumstances through prayer and prayer war. To fulfil the work of mission, we need greater cooperation between mission workers and intercessors. The intercessors will no longer stay at the home base; they will become forward troops, going out in the front line and breaking up the enemy ground. Today we are sending out teams of intercessors to unreached peoples and closed countries, so that they can clear the way for Bible translators, evangelists, and church planters.

Become a global intercessor for world evangelisation! Put a map of the world up in your prayer room. Make a list of the countries that are still closed to Christian work. I have a list like this, and during the last few years I have had many occasions to be thankful. Countries such as Albania and Mongolia have been opened for evangelism. As prayer tools use *Operation World*, a day-to-day guide to praying for the world, by Patrick Johnstone; or *Unreached Peoples* prayer profiles.

Start a prayer group in your church for unreached peoples. To begin with, it is best to get the church to adopt a particular group of unreached people. The church then pray for their unreached adopted family. The next step is to send out a team to the area, to pray and to reconnoitre. When the first contacts are made, the church then looks for mission workers, for whom they will afterwards be responsible, to send out as missionaries to their unreached people.

Spiritual front lines – the 10/40 window

Dr David Barrett, editor of the World Christian Encyclopedia, is working on a survey of where the unreached peoples are situated, where the most unevangelised of the major cities are, and where the closed countries are, to build up a picture of what still remains to be done in order to fulfil the task of mission. When he assembled all this information on his computer mapping system, he found that there was a 'window' lying roughly between the tenth and fortieth degrees of north latitude, and stretching from west to east across the eastern hemisphere. It is a rectangle that includes North Africa, the Middle East, India and Burma. In the East, it takes in Southeast Asia, parts of China, North Korea and Japan, Mongolia, the former Soviet republics of central Asia, Turkey, and Albania.

Dr Barrett says:

> 'That is our remaining task. Within these frontiers reside at least ninety-five percent of the world's unreached peoples – including all unevangelised megapeoples.'

Commenting on this in his book *The Last of the Giants*, George Otis jnr. says:

> 'Here we are faced with a challenge of enormous proportions. For lying within the frame of this strategic territory are the central headquarters of virtually every major non-Christian religious system on earth: Buddhism, Communism, Confucianism, Hinduism, Islam, Shintoism and Taoism. Only the corporate offices of materialism lie outside its borders.'

Here we have the spiritual battlefield of the 1990s. In the centre of the 10/40 window lie Iran and Iraq. The scene could not be more dramatic: the final scenario of the End Time will be played out in the ancient kingdoms of Persia and Babylon, where the princes of the gods of Persia and Babylon still cling to power. George Otis says:

> 'The serpent of Eden has established a global command and control center atop the oily residue of the Garden's once flourishing vegetation and animal life. The Bible alludes to such concentration of demonic authority as "seats" and they are not friendly to the purposes of God.'

Discipling nations

The Great Commission gives a calling to disciple nations. *'Therefore go and make disciples of all nations'* (Matthew 28:19). We have not discipled a nation until the majority of the population are dedicated disciples of Jesus Christ. There are nations with such a strong church growth that we can soon expect a majority of born-again Christians. South Korea is one country on the way to becoming a Christian nation.

We cannot disciple nations just by preaching within the four walls of a church. We need the teaching of Christian principles that can be applied in all areas of society. We need Christians in politics and the civil service, in education, business, and farming, in the media, in the arts, and so on. I tell Christians to take responsibility as if they were elected into power, but never to reach for positions of human might, but always to be willing to serve. God will use us to turn nations around. We have a desire to crown Jesus Lord in all the earth, and in every sphere of society.

The opportunity of discipling nations has arrived, at a time when everything has collapsed in the former Communist countries. The economy has been driven to rock bottom. Education, the care of the sick, and the system of law, are not functioning. The new regimes are asking desperately for help, and Christian contributions of help are welcomed. There are countries today where Christians are involved in the rebuilding of a nation. Some come to win people for God and to build churches. Others come to teach about the family and to build up the idea of the family, which has been laid in ruins. Others again are involved in building up schools, medical work, and the legal system. Where free enterprise has been prohibited for many years, Christian businessmen instruct former Communists on how to start businesses.

Before Jesus comes back, I expect a demonstration of his Kingdom in cities and nations. The gospel of the kingdom will be preached to all nations, and then the end will come. I expect the gospel of the kingdom to be both preached and demonstrated as a foretaste of the coming kingdom. To prepare for his coming is to prepare the nations for his rule. I expect God's glory to be manifested in some nations in such a way that he will establish a testimony to an unbelieving world to show what his kingdom is all about.

3. The Restoration of Israel

A prophetic understanding of God's plan for Israel is a key to understanding the End Time. If the Israel piece is laid in the right place in the End Time jigsaw puzzle, then all the other pieces will fit into their right places.

To enable us to understand our calling to the Jews, we must see clearly what God is doing for their restoration. This comprises three events:

1. **The restoration of the land.** *'Be not afraid, O land; be glad and rejoice'* (Joel 2:21). Little by little, Israel is recovering the land promised to the fathers. So far she has recovered 25 percent of it, and therefore the complete fulfilment of the promise is still to come.

2. **The return of the Jews to Israel.** Immigration to Israel has gone ahead, so that at present there are about 4 million Jews in Israel. But throughout the world there are about 16 million Jews, and the restoration is not fulfilled until all of them have come back to Israel. *'I will gather them to their own land, not leaving any behind'* (Ezekiel 39:28).

3. **The spiritual restoration of the Jews.** The dead bones will live; the Spirit will be poured out upon them. They will receive a new heart and enter into a new covenant. They

will recognise their Messiah and receive him as their King. This spiritual restoration has not yet happened, but we trust in God's promises and we shall follow them through to full restoration; following them through to salvation is like following a sinner through to salvation. They are the first nation with the promise that the whole nation will be saved and come into the kingdom of God. If you do not have faith in the salvation of the number one nation to be saved, how can you have faith for your own nation to be saved?

When will all Israel be saved? I have been brought up with the teaching that it will happen after the Church has been taken away in the Rapture. But Paul says, *'For if their rejection is the reconciliation of the world, what will their acceptance be but life from the dead?'* (Romans 11:15). In both their rejection and their acceptance they will influence the world and the Church; in fact, their acceptance will be like life from the dead in the Church. When born-again, Spirit-filled rabbis start teaching from the New Testament with all the deep insight that they have into the Old Testament, it will add a new dimension and bring resurrection life to nearly-dead churches. Today, I believe that Israel will be saved before the Rapture takes place, and before Jesus comes back. We will together complete the great commission and bring in the last harvest before Jesus comes. We are living in a time when the Lord has started to bring in the first-fruits of Israel. More Jews have come to believe in Yeshua as their Messiah than ever before in history; today there are Messianic congregations in the cities of Israel.

A gradual restoring of Israel is accompanied by a gradual outpouring of the Spirit over the earth. When David Ben-Gurion together with a group of other immigrants returned to Israel, the spiritual outpouring began which led to the historic Pentecostal awakening. In step with the great period of immigration in 1948–51, there was also a considerable outpouring of the Spirit throughout the world. While there is much that still remains outstanding in the process of restoring Israel, it means that there is also much still outstanding in the fulfilment of Joel's prophecy about the outpouring of the Spirit on all people.

The great exodus from the land of the north

The prophets foretold a great exodus of Jews from the land of the north in the End Time (Jeremiah 16:14–16). They will be fished home to Israel and they will be hunted home. The fishermen are those who call the Jews to go home to Israel, while they have been hunted home by such men of war as Hitler, Stalin and Khomeini. Jeremiah speaks of a great exodus from the land of the north, compared to which the exodus from Egypt will seem insignificant. The return from Babylon in Daniel's time never surpassed the exodus from Egypt, so there remains a great exodus still prophesied for the future.

The exodus from the land of the north is set in the context of the coming of Messiah (Jeremiah 23:5–8). Before the Jews can recognise Jesus as their Messiah, the Lord must first perform some preparatory miracle, which will lead them into believing in God's power and glory. The miracle of the release of the Jews from the Soviet Union will make it easier for the Jews to believe in the miracle of Jesus being their Messiah. Exodus II will be God's great trumpet blowing and declaring: 'Jesus the Messiah is returning to earth!'

The union of the Church with Israel

The prophet Ezekiel saw Judah's stick and Ephraim's stick united to become a single stick of wood in the Lord's hand.

> *'They will become one in my hand ... I will make them one nation in the land ... There will be one king over all of them and they will never again be two nations or be divided into two kingdoms.'* (Ezekiel 37:15–23)

Jesus referred to Ezekiel's vision of Judah and Ephraim, who would become one.

> *'I have other sheep that are not of this sheep pen. I must bring them also. They too will listen to my voice, and there shall be one flock and one shepherd.'* (John 10:16)

Jesus was speaking to his Jewish disciples and telling them that he would be calling other sheep who did not belong to the Jewish sheep pen: that is, us Gentiles who have heard the shepherd's voice and have been called together in the Church. But the shepherd will bring these two sheep pens together so that there will be one shepherd, one flock and one kingdom. We Christians can identify ourselves with Ephraim, who was the son of Joseph, born in Egypt to the daughter of an Egyptian priest who served false gods. Ephraim would never have been accepted as Jewish under present-day immigration rules; to be accounted a Jew it is now necessary to have a Jewish mother. Even though Ephraim was a Gentile, he was grafted into Abraham's blessed family tree through the patriarch Jacob, who pronounced a very special blessing on Ephraim: *'His descendants shall become a multitude of nations'* (Genesis 48:19 RSV). The phrase *'multitude of nations'* in Hebrew is *melo' hagoyim* which can properly be translated as *'the fullness of the Gentiles'*. This phrase only occurs in one other place in the Bible, where Paul uses it in Romans 11:25 *'... until the full number* (fullness) *of the Gentiles has come in. And so all Israel will be saved'*.

Christians and Jews are on the way to uniting. A spiritually born-again Israel will come together with a renewed Church and become one flock and one kingdom under Christ the Shepherd. In order for this process of union to happen, we need meeting-places where Jews and Christians can meet together.

Ezekiel saw that the miracle of union would take place in the Lord's hand. The two sticks of wood became one in his hand. The hand of the Lord, in the Bible, is a description of God intervening and acting in history. He brought the children of Israel out of Egypt with a strong and mighty hand: *'The Lord's hand was with them'* (Acts 11:21). The meeting-place for Christians and Jews is when God acts in history and fulfils the prophetic word.

We are living in a time when the Lord is bringing the Jews home from the dispersion, and Jews from the former Soviet Union are returning to the promised land. In this they are helped by Gentiles and inhabitants of the coastlands, who will bring them home in ships of Tarshish (Isaiah 60:9). Through prophetic visions and messages, Christians from all over the world have been prepared for the great exodus of Jews from the former Soviet Union, and they are prepared to help them with transport and accommodation while they are on their way to Israel. The church to which I belong has three times received Russian Jews on their way home from St Petersburg to Israel. We have known about our receiving of Russian Jews ever since March 1982, when the Lord revealed these things to a group of praying people who came into prophetic enlightenment and received a common revelation of Exodus II. When Christians serve Jews who are returning home by buses, ships and aircraft, meeting-places are naturally created for Christians and Jews. Christians are working today together with officers of the Jewish Agency to help returning Jews. In these meeting-places, prejudices between Jews and Christians are broken down. The Jews remember from history all the evil that Christians have done to them during the crusades and the Inquisition. They have not known that there are Christians who love them and are willing to serve them.

The prophetic word is a natural meeting-place between Jews and Bible-believing Christians. I have on many occasions heard Jewish politicians and officials quoting from the prophets and showing how the words of the prophets are being fulfilled. We quote the same Bible passages and together observe how they are being fulfilled. This provides us with a natural topic of conversation when we meet. Christians who are blind to the prophetic word, and who do not get to hear prophetic preaching in their churches, are denied this common platform with the Jews.

Prayer and worship are also meeting-places for Christians and Jews. Jews are sensitive to the spiritual dimension. They are aware of the presence of God. I have been many times to Israel in connection with intercessors' conferences and prayer journeys, and it has happened that totally secularised Jews have had occasion to come in. They have noticed and commented on the presence of God. When Christians and Jews have worked together to bring Russian Jews home to Israel, they have met in prayer gatherings. It is in worship singing that the real point of contact can be seen. Christian renewal has brought with it joyful worship singing, when the words of Scripture are sung and hands are lifted in praise; sometimes there is dancing. This lies very close to Israeli folk-music, which is often taken from the Bible. They dance to their folk-music and they dance in their synagogues. I have seen old Jewish men doing dance-steps in the synagogue at the Feast of Tabernacles, with a grandchild on one arm and a Torah scroll held in the other hand. Christians who are strangers to prayer and worship singing do not have this common meeting-place with the Jews.

A decisive meeting-place is in standing together in times of danger and persecution. Anti-semitism is again on the increase in the world, and it can increase to such an extent that it becomes necessary for us to hide Jews in our homes to protect them from persecutors. New Age groups say that they are helping Mother Earth to be released from negative powers. They proclaim the passing of the old order and all who support it, namely Jews and fundamentalist Christians.

The New World Order has brought nations together in imposing sanctions on countries such as Iraq, Libya and Serbia. One day, the weapon of sanctions will be raised against Israel. *'On that day, when all the nations of the earth are gathered against her, I will make Jerusalem an immovable rock for all the nations'* (Zechariah 12:3). Jews are never going to trust Christians completely until Christians have had the opportunity to show that they are ready to risk their lives to save Jews in their hour of danger. Christians need to have the same identification with the Jews, the chosen people of God, as Ruth the Moabite had with Naomi her mother-in-law:

'Your people will be my people and your God my God. Where you die I will die, and there I will be buried. May

213

the Lord deal with me, be it ever so severely, if anything
but death separates you and me.' (Ruth 1:16–17)

A liberal theologian has accused Bible-believing Christians
who support Israel of having a Holocaust theology. 'You
believe that the Jews will be hunted back to Israel by persecution. When the Jews return to Israel you believe that two-
thirds of them will perish and only one-third will survive the
holocaust in their own land' (Zechariah 13:8–9). How do you
answer that accusation? Do we have a 'Holocaust theology'?
Will the Lord allow the Jews to come back in order to see
them perish in the promised land? I do not believe that. What
about the two-thirds that will perish? In a time of greatest
danger for Israel, when the whole world turns against them,
Christians will prove themselves to be united with the Jews in
accordance with Ruth's confession. Many will come to Israel
and offer themselves as human shields. Before the Gulf War,
President Saddam Hussein of Iraq took all foreigners as hos-
tages and prevented them from leaving Iraq. He used them as
human shields. Once again the world will hear about human
shields, but this time it will be Christians offering themselves
of their own free will. Many of them will perish. One day
another Yad Vashem memorial will be built in Jerusalem, this
time in memory of millions who died in Israel or in their own
nations confessing themselves to be citizens of the Commonwealth of Israel. What will provoke the Jews to jealousy is that
Christians will be willing to die to protect them. In the
meeting-place of common persecution and suffering, Jews and
Christians will be joined together for the rest of history.

It is at the cross that the enmity between Jews and Gentiles
has been broken down. We need a meeting-place of reconciliation. We Christians bear the blame for everything that
Christians through the centuries have done against the Jews
living in our countries. The Jews carry an unhealed wound, a
memory of annihilation borne for life. They find it hard to
forgive. First of all it is when we come together and meet the
Lamb of God, who takes away the sin of the world, that there
can be a reconciliation between us. After we have met at the

cross, then we can become one new man, the new world-citizen.

Foreigners will rebuild your walls (Isaiah 60:10)

After every great exodus, when God's own people have returned to the promised land, the Gentiles have given them gifts towards the building of the tabernacle, the Temple, Jerusalem, and the land. When the Jews came out of Egypt, the women were told to ask their Egyptian neighbours for articles of silver and gold, and the Lord made the Egyptians favourably disposed to them, so that they did not need to come out with empty hands (Exodus 3:22). Cyrus king of Persia became the instrument of rebuilding Jerusalem after the Babylonian captivity. Cyrus, as a Gentile king, made a proclamation throughout the kingdoms of the earth that the God of heaven had appointed him to rebuild Jerusalem.

> *'And the people of any place where survivors* [of the Jews] *may now be living are to provide him with silver and gold, with goods and livestock, and with freewill offerings for the temple of God in Jerusalem.'* (Ezra 1:4)

The prophetic reckoning of time began in Daniel's time from the date of the issuing of the decree to restore and rebuild Jerusalem (Daniel 9:25).

Now, before our eyes, the latest exodus is taking place, with the Jews returning to Israel from the former Soviet Union and from the four corners of the earth. Jerusalem will again be built up. This time, however, the rebuilding is taking on a whole new dimension. Jerusalem is now going to be restored to become an international spiritual, cultural, and economic centre. We are now going to make it known throughout the earth that we, as the Church of God, have understood that it is God's calling to us to help Israel to rebuild Jerusalem so as to prepare the way for the return of Messiah: *'For the Lord will rebuild Zion and appear in his glory'* (Psalm 102:16).

Jerusalem as an international centre

God's word says that Jerusalem will become an international spiritual centre:

> '... *and peoples will stream to it* [Jerusalem]. *Many nations will come and say, "Come, let us go up to the mountain of the Lord, to the house of the God of Jacob. He will teach us his ways, so that we may walk in his paths. The law will go out from Zion, the word of the Lord from Jerusalem."'*
> (Micah 4:1–2)

When praying people come to Jerusalem from many different nations to pray together with Israeli Jews who believe in the Messiah, they join in the rebuilding of Jerusalem as an international spiritual centre. *'My house will be called a house of prayer for all nations'*, said Jesus of the temple in Jerusalem. Jerusalem will be the centre of the global prayer network.

Since the beginning of the 1980s, Christians from many countries have been coming each year to celebrate the Feast of Tabernacles in Jerusalem at the same time as the Jews are celebrating this feast. They are working together to prepare Jerusalem for the great Hosanna-feast when the city will welcome its Messiah and worship its King in Jerusalem.

> *'Then the survivors from all the nations that have attacked Jerusalem will go up year after year to worship the King, the Lord Almighty, and to celebrate the Feast of Tabernacles.'*
> (Zechariah 14:16)

Then there will again be heard in the streets of Jerusalem

> *'the sounds of joy and gladness, the voices of bride and bridegroom, and the voices of those who bring thank-offerings to the house of the Lord, saying, "Give thanks to the Lord Almighty, for the Lord is good; his love endures for ever."'*
> (Jeremiah 33:11)

When Jesus said farewell to Jerusalem, he said, *'You will not see me again until you say, "Blessed is he who comes in the name of the Lord"'* (Matthew 23:39). Jesus will not come back until Jerusalem has learnt how to welcome the Messiah. We prepare for his coming by working together so that the worship of Jesus grows and spreads through Jerusalem.

The prophet Isaiah prophesied that Jerusalem would become an international commercial centre.

> *'Your gates will always stand open, they will never be shut, day or night, so that men may bring you the wealth of the nations – their kings led in triumphal procession. For the nation or kingdom that will not serve you will perish.*
>
> (Isaiah 60:11–12)

The wealth of nations is the pride of the nations, the best a nation is able to produce and in which it is leading the world: the banking industry and the watches from Switzerland, Volvo cars and Ericsson telephones from Sweden, electronic products from Japan, tea from Sri Lanka and coffee from Brazil. All will be brought in through the financial centres of Jerusalem, which will be open 24 hours a day so as to be able to serve people in every time-zone of the world.

When Christian businessmen come in trade delegations representing their country in helping Israel to create work opportunities for Jewish immigrants from the former Soviet Union or from Ethiopia, they take part in the rebuilding of Jerusalem as a global centre of commerce. These trade delegations of Christians are clearing the way for a time when every country is going to come with its Head of State and its official trade delegation to participate, through Jerusalem, in international trade, in somewhat the same way as heads of government nowadays travel to the European Community headquarters in Brussels.

So that Jerusalem can be prepared for the coming of the King, we pray and work to enable Jerusalem to become an international financial centre of the kingdom of God. Up to now, Satan has had his power-base in the world economy, and the world centres of finance have been strongholds of Mammon in the spirit of Babylon, where pride, witchcraft and rebellion against God have prevailed. The Lord has begun to shake the financial strongholds of Mammon in all countries of the world, so as to guide the economic streams in the direction he has determined, that is, towards Jerusalem. The Lord will also be lighting a fire of purification in Israel's economy, dealing severely with pride, unrighteousness, Freemasonry, and the worship of false gods (Malachi 3:1–5).

Linking through a new trading perspective

About 400 Christian businessmen came from 29 nations in June 1992 to develop trading links and to interact with Israeli businessmen, to assist Israel in the job-creating process arising from the Aliyah (immigration). The event was held under the auspices of the International Christian Chamber of Commerce, and this is what the leader, Gunnar Olsson, said when he introduced the conference to Israeli politicians and leaders:

> 'There is an increasing trend among the nations not to support Israel. With our trade delegations we are the first-fruits from our nations who will stand against all the powers seeking to boycott Israel. We position ourselves firmly against the fear of co-operation with Israel in the market-place. We are looking beyond the greater markets such as the European Common Market, the United States of America and Asia, to the coming Kingdom. This is a rational business position based upon what we perceive is the greatness of Israel and its dynamics presently demonstrated through the Aliyah. This will result in Israel becoming the *gem* among the nations. It is also consistent with God's calling for Israel, to become a blessing for the nations.'

Jesus Christ's world government

Jesus Christ is coming back as the King of kings and Lord of lords. In his kingly might he is already bringing representatives from every people together in unity in his Church, so that later he will bring them together in unity in his kingdom.

> *'He will judge between the nations and will settle disputes for many peoples. They will beat their swords into ploughshares and their spears into pruning hooks. Nation*

will not take up sword against nation, nor will they train for war any more.' (Isaiah 2:4)

Jesus will come to take the position of an international judge with jurisdiction to settle disputes between states. A world government is seen by many as an important step towards a stable world peace. Jesus' world government is the only one that can carry this out. His peace comes through reconciliation taking place between peoples.

The New World Order is about to take shape

Today we are hearing the world's most powerful political leader use the expression 'The New World Order' in his speeches. Pat Robertson in his book *The New World Order* comes to the conclusion that for the past 200 years there has been a deliberate secret plan for the establishment of a new world organisation. This is the programme in the minds of those who govern the world behind the scenes. The vision is to gather the world's economy into a single monetary system and by this means to control that economy. In the course of history, national governments have been undermined, so that there will in the end be no way out for the nations other than to join in the world government. This purpose is on its way to being achieved by giving market forces a greater influence over governments than they have previously had. The idea is to create peace in the world by gathering the whole earth into a common forum. Robertson says that he is convinced that those who work for the New World Order are deliberately working to destroy the Christian faith.

Working for the Commonwealth of Israel

Paul said that we Gentiles were in the past excluded from the commonwealth of Israel, but Jesus became our peace, we were reconciled through the cross, and he made both Jews and Gentiles citizens in the commonwealth of Israel (Ephesians 2:12–19). How could we become citizens of the commonwealth of Israel? The disciples asked Jesus after his resurrection: *'Lord, are you at this time going to restore the kingdom to*

Israel?' (Acts 1:6). What kind of a kingdom were they asking for? It will not be a national state just for Israel. When the Messiah comes in his kingdom, Israel and Jerusalem will be the centre of an international group of states, a Messianic federation of nations. Isaiah the prophet saw the beginning of such a Messianic federation of three nations: Egypt, Israel, and Assyria (Iraq):

> *'In that day Israel will be the third, along with Egypt and Assyria, a blessing on the earth. The Lord Almighty will bless them, saying, "Blessed be Egypt my people, Assyria my handiwork, and Israel my inheritance.'*

(Isaiah 19:24–25)

I do not want to be a negative person spending all my time opposing the One World Government – certainly I will oppose it, but I want to do it in a positive way by having a Kingdom of God vision for another way of joining nations to one another. God's plan for your nation is threatened by the New World Order and the United States of Europe that is taking shape out of the European Community.

No country can any longer be independent of other countries. My nation can never exist as a nation cut off from other nations. I am praying and working for a highway of holiness and spiritual, economic and cultural linking between my nation and Jerusalem. Already we can look forward to the coming capital city of the Kingdom. God has a special plan for the five Nordic nations, all of which have the cross in their national flags. There is a strong, natural affinity between these peoples. We are going to be even more blessed by being linked with Israel and with other countries that also identify themselves with Israel. We do not need to belong to the rich nations' club. We would be more blessed by God if we linked our future with Israel and with the poor countries of Africa, Asia and South America, which are the least welcome in the European Community. Jesus demanded the ends of the earth as his possession (Psalm 2:8). Which countries would this mean? Those lying farthest away from Israel. This is where I expect the freeing of the earth to begin from. I have a vision of the beginning of the Commonwealth of Israel which will include the Nordic countries, countries in Africa, Australia, New Zealand, Alaska, Canada, South Africa and Argentina.

That assumes that every one of these countries comes to experience a massive harvest of people, leading to large numbers coming to believe in Jesus. It also assumes a strong prophetic conscience, and that there will be in these countries prophetic churches that can guide their country's leaders through the prophetic word. Yes, it assumes that these countries will have Prime Ministers and Presidents who are born again, spirit-filled, and Bible-believing.

If one day I have to risk my life by refusing to take the mark of the beast on my forehead, I want to do it by having a positive dream, a dream about the Commonwealth of Israel, a Messianic federation of states joined with Israel to be a platform for the World Government of Jesus the Messiah when he returns.

The proclamation of welcome to the bridegroom

The Bible ends with Jesus saying: *'Yes, I am coming soon.'* The bride's answer is given by John: *'Amen. Come, Lord Jesus'* (Revelation 22:20). This welcome to Jesus has been spoken out only by certain Christians, often those who have suffered persecution and could see no other way out than that Jesus should come. But it should surely be enough, considering the bride's great love for the bridegroom, for her to burst out with this cry of welcome from her inmost heart?

One of the things that needs to be done as a preparation for the coming of Jesus is that, throughout the world, the Bride of Christ should say her 'Welcome!' to the bridegroom. The coming of Christ is not going to be a seizing of an unwilling bride. When a wedding is to be celebrated, the bride must first have given her unequivocal 'yes'. Only then can the parties agree on a date, decide the place for the wedding, invite the guests and sew the bridal gown.

Jesus said his 'yes' long ago in Gethsemane, when he knew that it was to cost him his life to purchase his Bride on the earth. The Bride Church must say her 'yes' while she is still in her home on earth.

The great desire of the Holy Spirit before the conclusion of his task is to hear the Bride proclaiming her welcome and willingly saying her 'yes'. During the time before the coming of Jesus, the Holy Spirit comes through the Elijah ministry, preparing the Bride Church so that she expresses her love and longing for the bridegroom, Christ, at the same time all over the world.

We can hasten the coming of the day of Jesus, among other ways, by getting the Bride to say her 'yes' and her welcome from the heart. During the past year I have on many occasions taught this, and have concluded church meetings by asking the whole church to stand and proclaim their welcome to Jesus in unison:

> JESUS, WE LOVE THE PROSPECT OF YOUR
> COMING.
> JESUS, MAY YOUR KINGDOM OF PEACE COME
> TO OUR WORLD.
> JESUS, WE LONG TO SEE YOU AS KING OVER
> THE WHOLE WORLD.
> THEREFORE, WE WILL DO THOSE THINGS
> THAT WILL BRING YOU BACK AS KING
> OVER THE WHOLE WORLD.
> JESUS, AS YOUR BLOOD-BOUGHT BRIDE WE
> SAY OUR WELCOME TO YOU.
> AMEN. COME, LORD JESUS!